CONTENTS

BASIC ESSENTIALS	6
SANDS, SEA AND SHORE *seascape sofa*	8
IKEBANA *Japanese-style rug*	12
FRUITY FOLLY *wild appliqué*	16
LITTLE WHITE TIES *transform your home*	20
SCATTERED FLOWERS *chair cover*	24
COLOR AND LIGHT *needlepoint mat*	27
HOLIDAY FUN CURTAIN *simply child's play*	30
INSTANT SEATING *comfort with style*	32
GEOMETRIC PERFECTION *cool summer mat*	34
PRISMATIC NET *triangular patch curtain*	37
A ROSE IS A ROSE *blind with a view*	38
BUTTERFLY PICNIC *embroidered damask*	40
BOUND WITH BOWS *pretty table set*	44
PROVENÇAL PICNIC SET *outdoor elegance*	46
LIGHT AS AIR *organdy placemats and napkins*	48
WHITE AS SNOW *for Scandinavian warmth*	50
BEDROOM PAGEANTRY *canopy curtains and cover*	52
RUG TRANSFORMATION *quick embroidered flowers*	55
CRADLED IN COMFORT *baby blue coordinates*	56
SPRINGTIME DREAM *tulips for collectors*	60
LACED HEADBOARD *stylish and sporty*	64
SUNNY DAYS *elegant deckchair set*	66
CELEBRATION TIME *setting the scene*	70
PATCHWORK CURTAIN *sunlit scenery*	72
LAZY DAYS *colorful hammock*	74
COLORFUL HARMONY *ribbons for a beautiful home*	76
STOCKISTS	80

INTRODUCTION

It is the finishing touches that turn a house into a home – items that you have made yourself, giving them an individuality that speaks volumes about your personal taste and character. The French excel in the art of adding little details and unexpected turns of design that transform a collection of assorted objects into a harmonious room, and this book contains a superb collection of things to sew for the home, all with a strong French flavor.

The items range from covers, cushions, curtains and rugs to bed and table linen, and all are designed with flair and imagination. There is something for virtually every taste, from the traditional to the ultra modern, and for every type of home, from a holiday cottage to a stylish town house.

Many of the projects, such as the dramatic and amusing canopy, duvet set and tabbed curtains on page 52, entail no more than straight seaming, others involve a variety of needlework skills ranging from simple patchwork and appliqué to embroidery, canvaswork and rugmaking. All are lavishly illustrated and fully and clearly explained, with drawings to illustrate particular points, so that you can't go wrong.

There are a few projects to challenge the more ambitious needlewoman, including a ravishingly pretty bedcover with matching pillowcases, embroidered with sprays of tulips, but the majority of the items in this book require no advanced skills. The very stylish finished appearance is due to the originality of the designs. You do not, for instance, need upholstery lessons to make the loose sofa cover and cushions which a French designer decorated with minimal embroideries to complement the wild seascape from her holiday home; or there is the patchwork curtain made from white cotton appliquéd with chintz squares – it looks marvelous but is very quick and straightforward to make.

So whether you have never made anything of this kind before or whether your home is already full of beautiful objects that you have sewn yourself, you will find plenty of things in these pages that are fun to make and that will enhance your surroundings.

French Chic

DECORATIVE HOME SEWING

100 IDEES
Ballantine Books · New York

Conceived, designed and produced by
Conran Octopus Limited
28-32 Shelton Street
London WC2 9PH

Editor: Diana Mansour
Contributing Editor: Hilary More
Art Editor: Caroline Murray
Illustrators: Paul Cooper, Coral Mula,
Prue Bucknell

Copyright © 1980, 1981, 1982, 1983, 1984, 1985, 1986 100 IDEES
Translation copyright © by 100 IDEES and Conran Octopus Limited
1987

All rights reserved under International Pan-American Copyright Conventions. Published in the United States by Ballantine Books, a division of Random House, Inc., New York, and simultaneously in Canada by Random House of Canada Limited, Toronto. Originally published in Great Britain by Conran Octopus Limited.

Library of Congress Catalogue Card Number 86 – 91630

ISBN: 0-345-34418-9

Manufactured in Hong Kong

First American Edition: May 1987

10 9 8 7 6 5 4 3 2 1

Acknowledgments (Photographer/Stylist)

title page M. Duffas/J. Schoumacher   4-5 N. Bruant/C. Lebeau
8-11 M. Duffas/J. Schoumacher   12-17 B. Maltaverne/C. Lebeau
20-22 M. Duffas/J. Schoumacher   23 above left M. Duffas/J. Schoumacher
23 above right and below P. Hussenot/J. Schoumacher   24-25 A. Bianchi/I. Garçon
27 G. de Chabaneix/A. Luntz   30-31 M. Duffas/J. Schoumacher
32-33 P. Hussenot/J. Schoumacher   34-35 D. Burgi/C. Lebeau
37-39 M. Duffas/J. Schoumacher   40-43 V. Assenat/J. Schoumacher
44-54 M. Duffas/J. Schoumacher   55 G. Bouchet/C. Lebeau
56-57 M. Duffas/J. Schoumacher   60-61 G. de Chabaneix/I. Garçon
64-71 M. Duffas/J. Schoumacher   72-73 N. Bruant/C. Lebeau
74-75 B. Maltaverne/C. Lebeau   76-77 M. Garçon/J. Schoumacher
78 above M. Duffas/J. Schoumacher   78 below M. Garçon/J. Schoumacher
79 M. Garçon/J. Schoumacher

BASIC ESSENTIALS

The techniques used in this book are all very straightforward, and the patterns are easy to use if you follow the methods for enlarging and transferring them as given below. Throughout, it is assumed that seams which are not enclosed will be edge-finished if the fabric tends to ravel and that ordinary open seams, described below, will be used unless it is otherwise stated in the pattern.

DRAWING UP FROM A GRID PATTERN

Use dressmakers' pattern paper which is printed in squares. Select a starting point on the pattern, then mark a corresponding point on the pattern paper. Find the adjacent point on the pattern and mark the same point on the paper. Continue in this manner. Where the lines are straight simply draw them with a ruler. On curved lines plot around the lines and join them up together freehand. Cut out the resulting pattern piece. To enlarge or reduce the pattern, draw up the shapes onto smaller or larger squares.

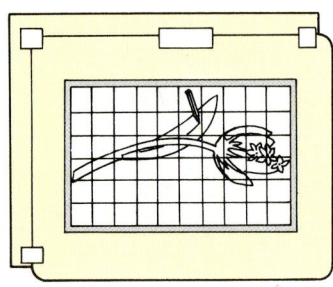

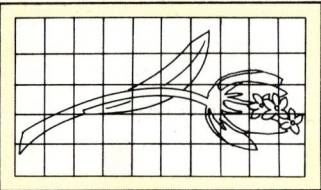

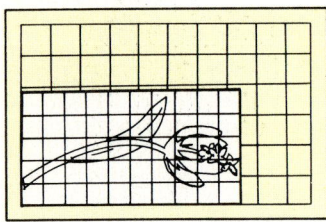

USING DRESSMAKERS' CARBON PAPER

Position the pattern paper centrally over the right side of the fabric and pin it to the fabric at each corner. Carefully slide a sheet of dressmakers' carbon paper carbon side down, between the pattern and the fabric. Mark over the design lines of the pattern with a pencil or tracing wheel.

SEAMS

Plain seam
Place the two fabric pieces with right sides together, raw edges even; pin and stitch together ⅝in (1.5cm) from the raw edges. Work a few stitches in reverse at each end to secure the threads.

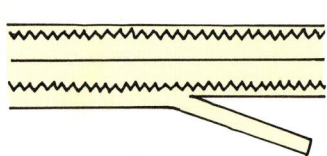

The simplest method of finishing the seam allowance edges is by zigzag stitching on a sewing-machine. Use a short, narrow stitch worked slightly in from the raw edge. If the fabric has a tendency to fray use a larger stitch and work over the raw edge. Where the fabric is fine turn under the raw edge and either zigzag stitch or straight stitch. If finishing by hand, overcast the raw edges: work from left to right, taking the thread diagonally over the edge and keeping the stitches about ⅛in (3mm) apart. If the fabric tends to fray, work a row of straight stitching first, then oversew over the edge. If the fabric is very heavy simply pink the edges using a pair of pinking shears.

Flat fell seam
This is a self-finishing seam that is very strong and distinctive. Place the two fabric pieces with right sides together and raw edges even; pin and stitch together ⅝in (1.5cm) from the raw edges. Press the seam allowance to one side. Trim down the lower seam allowance to ¼in (6mm). Fold the upper seam allowance over, enclosing the lower seam allowance. Press the folded allowance flat against the fabric; pin and stitch close to the folded edge.

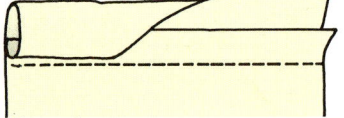

French seam
This is a self-finishing seam. Place the two fabric pieces with wrong sides together; pin and stitch ¼in (6mm) from the raw edges. Press the seam open. Refold with right sides together; pin and stitch ⅜in (1cm) from the seamed edge.

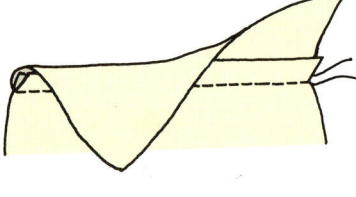

FASTENINGS

How to insert a zipper
Pin and tack the seam into which the zipper is to be inserted. Stitch in from each, or from one, end of the seam, leaving an opening the same length as the zipper. Press

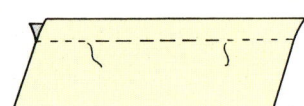

the tacked seam open. Place the zipper face down over the seam allowances with the bottom stop ⅛in (3mm) beyond the tacking at one side and with the teeth centered over the tacked seam. Tack in place through all layers ¼in (6mm) on either side of the teeth. Turn to the right side. Stitch the zipper in place using a zipper foot on the sewing-machine or back-stitch by hand, following the tacking lines at the sides and pivoting the stitching at the bottom corners or at both ends.

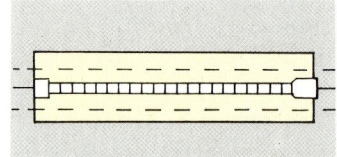

Stitched buttonholes
Mark the buttonhole length the same diameter as the button. Tack all around the buttonhole position and then cut along the marked buttonhole line, along a single thread of fabric, through all layers. Overcast the cut edges with small stitches. Either using buttonhole thread or ordinary sewing thread, secure the thread end inside the two fabrics and work along the slit in buttonhole stitch, working a straight bar of stitches at the end. Continue along the opposite side and work another vertical bar at the opposite end. Fasten off.

Bias strips
To cut the fabric on the bias fold the fabric so that the selvage (warp threads) lies exactly parallel to the weft threads. The fold formed is the true cross. Cut along the fold and then cut the bias strips parallel to this edge.

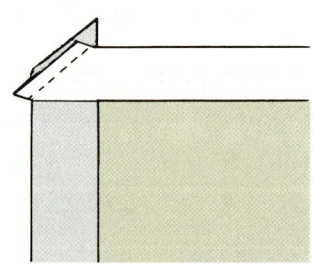

Mark off the strips using pins or a marking pen and cut out. To join strips together, place two strips with right sides together on the straight of grain, as shown, and stitch together taking ¼in (6mm) seams. Trim off points level with side edges and press seam open.

BASIC ESSENTIALS

MITERING THE CORNERS

Mitering a fabric band

Fold the fabric band in half lengthwise, raw edges together. Fold up the raw edges in line with folded edge and press. Cut along the fold lines. Repeat at the opposite end of strip, but so the diagonal edge is facing in the opposite direction. Repeat with all strips. Unfold two adjoining

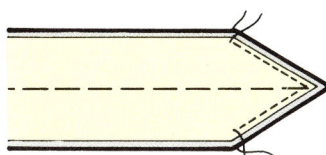

strips and place with right sides together and pointed ends matching. Pin and stitch the end, beginning and ending the stitching ⅝in (1.5cm) from each end of the seam. Trim and turn to the right side, refolding the strip in half. Repeat, to form each mitered corner. Place one edge to main piece with right sides together; pin and stitch. Turn under remaining edge of band and slipstitch over previous stitches on the wrong side.

Mitering binding

Unfold one edge of binding and place against the raw fabric edge. Pin and stitch in place along first side up to the seam allowance at the turning point. Press up the binding over the stitched side at a 45 degree angle. Stitch the next

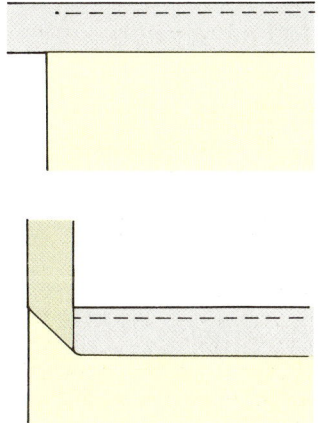

side beginning at the turning point. Trim and turn binding over the raw edge to the wrong side folding the excess binding on both sides into miters. Slipstitch remaining folded edge of binding over previous stitches on the wrong side. If the binding is wide, stitch across the corner on the right side of the fabric before turning the binding over the raw edge. Trim and press open. Then pleat the excess fabric into a miter on the wrong side.

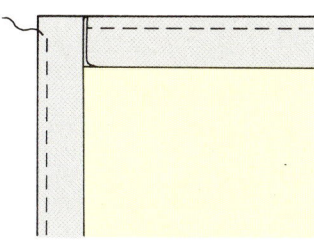

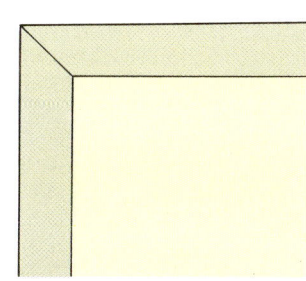

MEASURING FOR CURTAINS

Always follow the fixing instructions that come with your chosen track or pole, but if you are curtaining on an existing track measure from the top of the track or pole or wire to the desired length and add on the stated allowances for hems and top fixing.

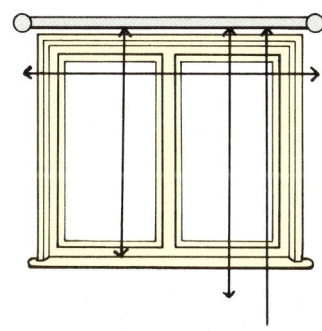

HAND STITCHES

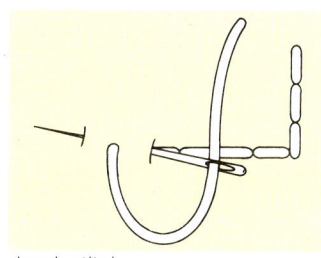
back stitch

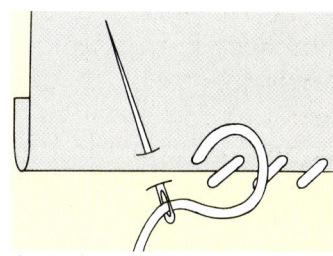
hemming stitch

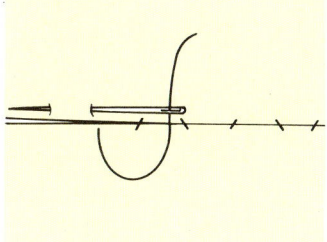
slipstitch

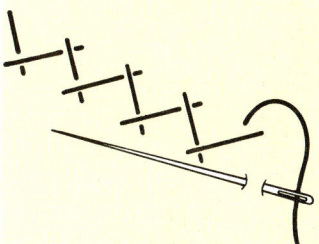
herringbone stitch

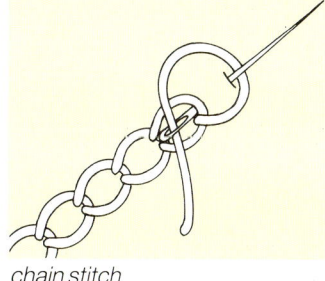
chain stitch

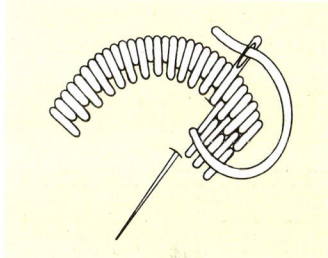
long and short stitch

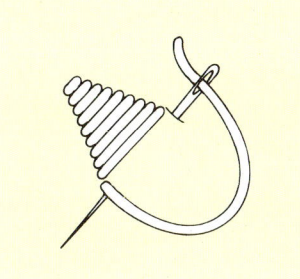
satin stitch

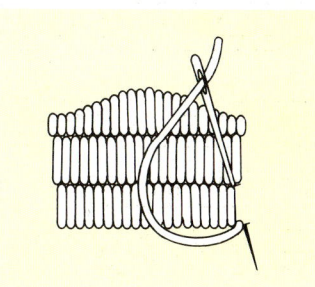
encroaching satin stitch

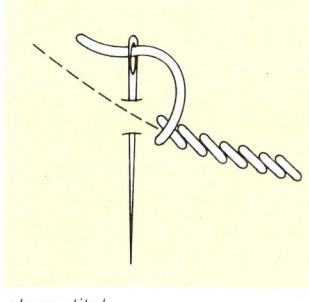
stem stitch

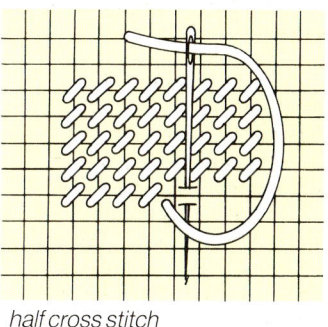
half cross stitch

7

SANDS, SEA AND SHORE

Minimal, single-color designs, as wild and charming as the dunes and grasses of a lonely seashore, are worked on fabric chosen to echo the colors of northern seas. The loose cover and cushions were made by designer Janick Schoumacher to complement the lovely scenery from the windows of her holiday home. The idea of breaking down the clear-cut line between inside and outside works very well, but the sofa could equally be used to set the scene for a room centered on a seascape picture.

Size: instructions show how to cut and fit the loose cover to your own sofa.

MATERIALS

Fabric – see below for quantity
12 skeins of DMC stranded cotton in white
Size 6 or 7 crewel needle
Large embroidery hoop
Zippers for cushion covers – about 4in (10cm) shorter than finished width of cushion
Six hooks and eyes
Matching thread
Dressmakers' carbon paper

DIRECTIONS

THE CUSHION COVERS

▪ Measure one of your cushions and cut three pieces for cushion fronts to this size plus 5/8in (1.5cm) seam allowance all around.
▪ Trace the designs from the photographs and enlarge them to the required dimensions. Transfer to fabric, using dressmakers' carbon paper.
▪ Work with fabric stretched in an embroidery hoop, moving it as necessary. Using the photographs as stitch guides, embroider the grass in stem stitch, sand in French knots (see page 36), and water and dunes in satin stitch and encroaching satin stitch. Three strands of thread are used throughout.
▪ When embroidery is complete, place each piece face downwards on a well padded surface and press it lightly, taking care not to crush the stitches.
▪ For each cushion back, cut a piece to the finished measurements plus 1¼in (3cm) on the width and 2½in (6cm) on the length. Cut in half across the width.
▪ Place back pieces with right sides together. Pin and tack together along the width, taking 5/8in (1.5cm) seam allowance. Stitch for 2 5/8in (6.5cm) from each side. Press seam open. Place zipper face down over seam, with teeth over tacked section. Pin, tack and then stitch from right side. Open zipper.
▪ Matching outer edges, pin and stitch cushion front and back pieces together around outer edges, taking 5/8in (1.5cm) seam allowance. Trim and edge-finish seam allowance. Turn cover right side out, insert the cushion and close the zipper.

THE LOOSE COVER

▪ To estimate fabric needed, it helps to draw chalk lines on a suitable floor space, the width of the fabric apart, and sketch in the shapes as you measure, bearing in mind matching stripes or patterns.
▪ Each part of the sofa is measured both ways, as shown in diagram, and measurements are written down. Except for front and arm panels, all pieces are cut out as rectangles, then trimmed and pin-fitted into place on sofa before stitching.
▪ On the fabric, mark out each rectangle, bearing in mind fabric design, then cut out each piece. Add 1½in (4cm) to any side which will form base hem, and 6in (15cm) tuck-in allowance to base of inside back and inside arms and to top and side edges of seat. Add 2in (5cm) to all other sides for fitting and seam allowances. Mark each piece with its name, and also the top and base.
▪ Mark center of sofa back, inside back and seat with a row of pins. Fit outside back in place first; place fabric on sofa, matching centers, and pin.
▪ Repeat with inside back, putting tuck-in allowance at base. Pin to outside back around back and sides.
▪ Pin inside and outside arms in place in the same way, with tuck-in allowance on inside arms. Pin arms to inside back, clipping into fabric allowance if necessary to gain a good curve.
▪ Pin seat in place to inside back and arms, with tuck-in allowance at back. Taper tuck-in allowance from nothing at sofa front to full depth at back of seat. Pin tuck-in allowances together around seat.
▪ Place tracing paper to front arm panel and carefully mark outline. Use as template, adding seam and hem allowances as before. Cut a matching pair of front arm panels.
▪ Arrange excess fabric around one arm front into evenly-spaced darts, then make opposite arm exactly the same. Pin front panels in place, again making sure that the shaping of the panels will look identical when sewn.
▪ Check that cover fits well then mark all seamlines with chalk. Remove cover from sofa; tack and stitch pieces together in same order as pinned, leaving one back corner seam open for about two-thirds of its length for fastenings.
▪ For strength, stitch each seam again just inside previous stitching. Trim seam allowances to ½in (1.2cm) and edge-finish.
▪ Face the back opening: snip into seam allowance at the top of the opening point up to the stitching. Cut a 3¼in (8cm) wide

seascape sofa

SANDS, SEA AND SHORE

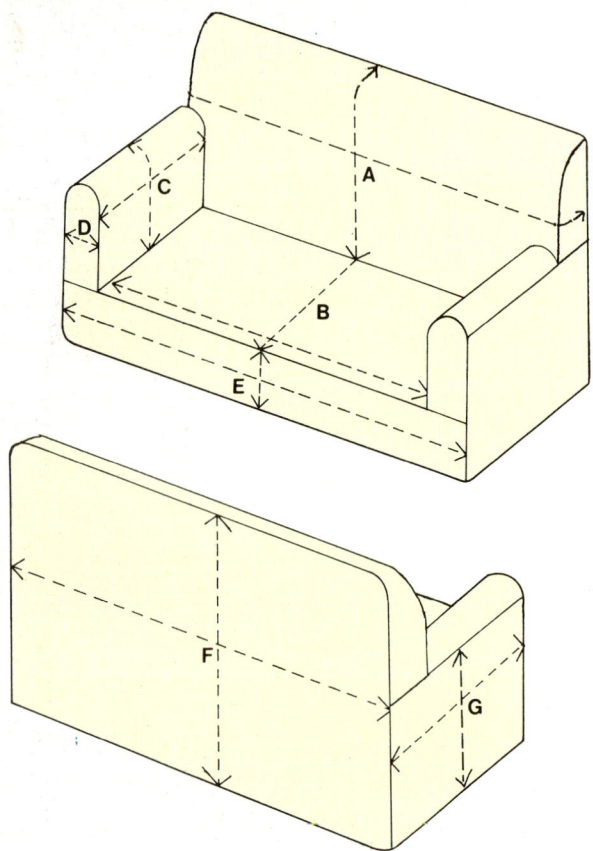

A Inside back

B Seat

C Inside arm (×2)

D Front arm panel (×2)

E Front panel

F Back

G Outside arm (×2)

Sofas differ widely in shape, and if yours has a thickly padded or clearly defined back, you may need an additional panel running up the sides and along the top of the back rest, joining the inside and outside back pieces. Similarly, if the arms extend beyond the seat section, the front arm panels must run from the top of the arms down to the floor, and the front panel will be correspondingly narrower.

strip of fabric twice the length of the opening. With opening held out straight, place strip with right side to wrong side of opening. Pin, tack and stitch, taking ⅝in (1.5cm) seam allowance. Turn in ⅝in (1.5cm) along remaining long edge of strip and bring over seam on right side of cover. Pin, tack and stitch in place. Fold facing to inside of cover. Stitch hooks and eyes into faced opening, spacing them evenly.

▪ Replace cover over sofa and measure for the front panel, across complete sofa front. Remove cover. Cut out one piece to this size, adding ⅝in (1.5cm) for seams and 1½in (4cm) for base hem. Pin, tack and stitch in place to seat, front arm panel and to outside arm at each side. Trim and finish seam allowances.

▪ Turn under a double 2cm (¾in) hem all round base edge of cover, so cover will just clear the floor. Pin, tack and stitch in place.

▪ Replace the cover over the sofa, pushing the tuck-in allowance down all around the seat. Add the cushions along the back.

SANDS, SEA AND SHORE

11

IKEBANA

This square rug, with its interplay of rich autumnal colors and rounded shapes, has a wonderful feeling of life and movement, like a split second taken from a juggling act. It was inspired by an antique Japanese textile, but its simple, almost abstract shapes would blend superbly into an uncluttered modern setting. If these colors are not suited to your decor, trace over the basic outlines and experiment with other colorways until you have found a combination that works. Even a very minor change, such as altering the color of some balls, perhaps to echo the color of a lamp base or some scatter cushions, could have a subtle but important effect, bringing the design into harmony with a room setting, without involving a great deal of extra preparation.

Size: approximately 55in × 55in (140cm × 140cm).

MATERIALS

60in × 60in (1.5m × 1.5m) of 4-gauge DMC rug canvas
DMC rug wool in ready-cut packs in the following quantities and colors: 85 packs beige 7143; 66 packs fawn 7520; 30 packs black; 24 packs red 7107; 19 packs pale pink 7120; 8 packs green 7384; 6 packs orange 7850; 5 packs yellow 7504; 4 packs ecru; 3 packs each of blue 7305 and gold 7505, and 2 packs pink 7202
Latchet rug hook
Wide masking tape
6⅞yd (6.2m) of 1½in (4cm) wide rug binding
Heavy duty sewing needle
Beige button thread or linen carpet thread
Note If the above rug yarn is unobtainable, refer to page 80.

DIRECTIONS

▦ The rug is knotted using a lachet hook (see overleaf), and each square on the chart represents one rug knot worked over one horizontal thread of canvas.
▦ To make each knot, take a cut strand of wool and fold it in half. Holding the two ends firmly, slip the wool over the hook, below the crook and latch, and insert the hook under a horizontal thread of canvas.
▦ Open the latch and insert the two ends of wool into the hook then closing the latch, pull the ends back under the canvas thread and through the loop.
▦ Pull the two ends to make a firm knot before moving onto the next. If one side of a knot is longer than the other, do not be tempted to trim the longer end as this will result in the finished rug having an uneven pile. Instead, remove the yarn and rework the knot.
▦ Before working the design, bind canvas edges with masking tape to prevent threads unravelling. Work row by row across the canvas, following chart for design and colors. Begin at the lower edge, approximately 4¾in (12cm) in from raw edge of canvas, and work upwards to top of chart, working in horizontal rows. Much of the background of the rug is worked in two colors in order to produce a more interesting, multicolored pile of either beige and fawn or beige and pink. It is important to stagger the position of the colors from row to row, rather like brickwork, in order to achieve a speckled effect instead of stripes.
▦ When knotting is complete, trim away surplus canvas, leaving

Japanese-style rug

IKEBANA

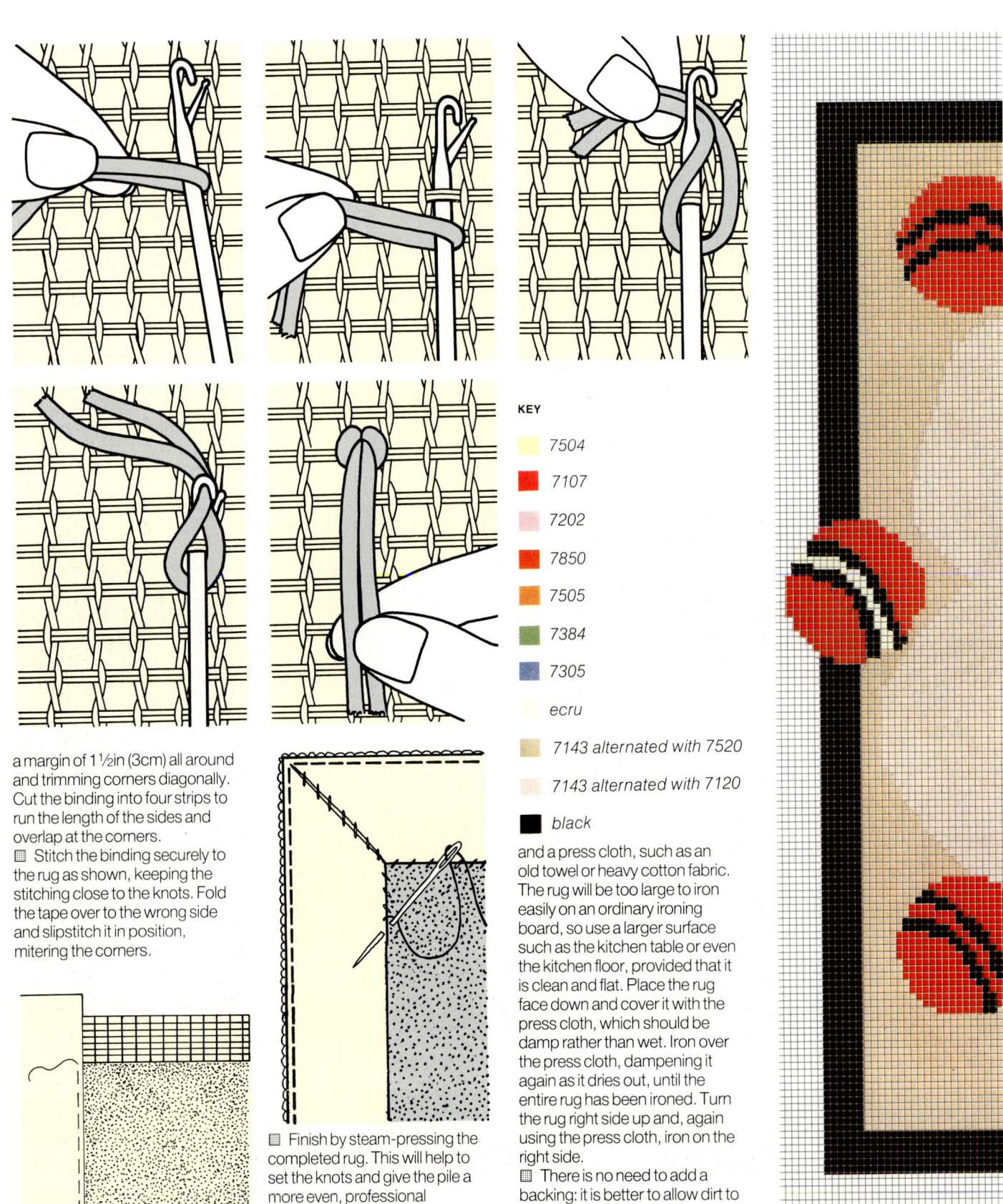

a margin of 1½in (3cm) all around and trimming corners diagonally. Cut the binding into four strips to run the length of the sides and overlap at the corners.
▦ Stitch the binding securely to the rug as shown, keeping the stitching close to the knots. Fold the tape over to the wrong side and slipstitch it in position, mitering the corners.

▦ Finish by steam-pressing the completed rug. This will help to set the knots and give the pile a more even, professional appearance. Use a steam iron and a press cloth, such as an old towel or heavy cotton fabric. The rug will be too large to iron easily on an ordinary ironing board, so use a larger surface such as the kitchen table or even the kitchen floor, provided that it is clean and flat. Place the rug face down and cover it with the press cloth, which should be damp rather than wet. Iron over the press cloth, dampening it again as it dries out, until the entire rug has been ironed. Turn the rug right side up and, again using the press cloth, iron on the right side.
▦ There is no need to add a backing: it is better to allow dirt to fall through to the floor.

KEY

- 7504
- 7107
- 7202
- 7850
- 7505
- 7384
- 7305
- ecru
- 7143 alternated with 7520
- 7143 alternated with 7120
- black

IKEBANA

15

FRUITY FOLLY

This eccentric tablecloth, decorated with a medley of outsize fruits, mugs and fans (to help you to keep cool on hot summer days) is guaranteed to put a keen edge on your appetite. If you enjoy hand sewing, you can appliqué the various motifs to the background fabric by hand, but if not, then they can easily be applied with a machine zigzag stitch. If you are really lucky you might be able to find a fabric with a pattern close to that of your china, to give the appliquéd mugs a trompe l'oeil effect.

Size: 80½in × 59in (202cm × 148cm).

MATERIALS

1¾yd (1.6m) of 48in (120cm) wide plain blue fabric
1¾yd (1.6m) of 45in (115cm) wide black and white check fabric
Assortment of different colored, plain and printed fabrics for appliqué
Odds and ends of broderie anglaise, broderie anglaise edging and braid for appliqué
Green embroidery cotton
Yellow and pink fabric paints
Matching thread

DIRECTIONS

▦ From check fabric cut out two pieces, each 64in × 20in (160cm × 50cm).
▦ Draw up the patterns for the motifs from the diagram. Cut out eight lemons from plain yellow fabric, three apples and three plums from plain green fabric. From plain orange fabric cut out seven 8in (20cm) diameter circles, for oranges. Cut out three large and four small strawberries from plain red fabric with stalks from plain green. Pin and tack the pieces to the background fabrics. Lay the stalks over the top of the strawberries and zigzag stitch in place. Embroider seeds in bullion knots in green embroidery cotton, as shown.
▦ Paint over the tops of the strawberries with yellow or pink paint, and fix according to manufacturer's instructions.
▦ From printed fabric cut out three mugs. Position braid around mug, as shown; pin, tack and zigzag stitch in place. From plain blue fabric cut out a large flower motif for each mug. Appliqué to each mug, as before.
▦ Make up two fans: cut out from printed fabric, then lay bands of broderie anglaise or second print fabric over the fan and zigzag stitch in place. Pin and tack broderie anglaise edging behind the curved outer edge of broderie anglaise fan.
▦ Trim blue fabric to 64in × 48in (160cm × 120cm). Lay it right side up on a flat surface and position all the motifs following the diagram, overlapping the outer edges where shown. Pin, tack and stitch in place close to the outer edge. Zigzag stitch around each motif, adding stalks to the apples.
▦ Appliqué shapes to each piece of check fabric in the same way following the diagram for positions.
▦ Pin, tack and stitch check fabric strips to either side of blue fabric with flat fell seams.
▦ Turn under a 2½in (6cm) hem all around outer edge, tuck under ⅜in (1cm), mitering the corners. Pin, tack and stitch hem in place.

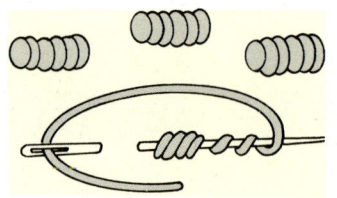

16

wild appliqué

FRUITY FOLLY

1 square = 2in x 2in

Raw edges will be covered by the stitching, but the pieces must first be tacked to the background fabric with the stitches running all around, fairly close to the edge. When machining the stalks, work up to each point, then raise the presser foot while the needle is in the down position and turn the fabric.

FRUITY FOLLY

1 square = 8in x 8in

LITTLE WHITE TIES

A novel, even rather outrageous way of changing the entire appearance of your home, these white covers, like dust sheets, could be hiding virtually anything: is that an antique Louis XV table or is it laminated plastic – who can say? And are the real owners relaxing on the Orient Express while sophisticated intruders make use of their abandoned house? If you are bored with your surroundings, or the colors are too warm and suffocating for summer, or your old chairs need a facelift but don't merit the full treatment, here's one way to create an air of mystery and impermanence, and at the same time to turn everyday furnishings into white, sculptured objects.

Sizes: tablecloth 79½in × 79½in (202cm × 202cm); fireplace and chair covers to fit individual requirements.

MATERIALS

FOR THE TABLECLOTH
5¾yd (5m) of 45in (115cm) wide bleached calico
Matching thread
11yd (10m) of ½in (13mm) wide white binding tape

FOR THE FIREPLACE
White cotton fabric – see below for quantity
Matching thread

FOR THE PLAIN CHAIR COVER
White cotton fabric – see below for quantity
Matching thread

FOR THE BLACK AND WHITE COVERS
White cotton fabric – see below for quantity
Black sewing cotton or black fabric painting pen
Matching thread

DIRECTIONS

THE FIREPLACE COVER

▪ If you prefer, you could make this summer cover in a pastel or chintz fabric, but do not use it when the fire is lit, even if it seems to hang well clear of the flames. The cover is made from six pieces: one for the top (shelf) of the mantelpiece, two outer (side) pieces, one top front and two side fronts. Measure the length and depth of the top (shelf) of the mantelpiece, then measure from the sides of the shelf down to floor level. Cut out a piece for the top, adding ¾in (2cm) to the back (wall) edge and ⅜in (1cm) to all other edges. Cut two side pieces, adding ¾in (2cm) to the back (wall) edges, 1½in (4cm) to the base (floor) edges and ⅜in (1cm) to all other edges. For the front, measure from shelf to floor and from outer side to inner (fireplace) side, for side pieces, and from inner side to side for front section. Cut side pieces, adding 1½in (4cm) to the base edges and ⅜in (1cm) to top and outer side edges. Cut out centre front, adding 1½in (4cm) to the base (floor) edge and ⅜in (1cm) to top edge.

▪ Pin, tack and stitch the outer sides to the top (shelf) piece, with right sides together and with plain seams, leaving ⅜in (1cm) unstitched at the front edges. Turn under a double ⅜in (1cm) hem along the entire back (wall) edge; pin, tack and stitch.

▪ For the fireplace front, cut 3¼in (8cm) wide strips of binding to run along both sides of front section and along inner (fireplace) side of each side section. Place each strip against the edge which is to be bound, with right sides together. Taking a 1¼in (2cm) seam allowance, pin, tack and stitch together. Turn under 1¼in (2cm) along remaining long edge of binding; bring binding over the raw edge and pin, tack and slipstitch to the back, covering the previous line of stitching. Bind remaining side edges in the same way.

▪ Lap bound edges of front over side sections: total width of

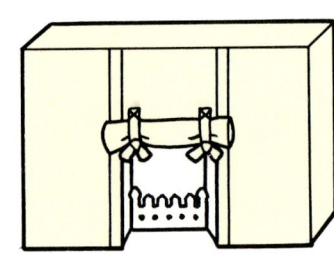

overlap ¾in (2cm) at each side. Pin, tack and stitch together down both sides of bound edge to the level of the top of the fireplace (inner edge).

▪ Cut out four strips, each 18in × 3¼in (46cm × 8cm), for tapes. Press in ⅜in (1cm) turnings all around, then fold each strip in half, with wrong sides together. Pin, tack and stitch all around each strip. Position two pairs of tapes on right and wrong side of center piece about 1¼in (3cm) above top of fireplace opening and 6in (15cm) in from either side edge. Stitch tape ends in place.

▪ Place front to mantelpiece side (top) piece, matching top seams to corners of front section; pin, tack and stitch together.

▪ Turn up a double ¾in (2cm) wide base hem all around cover; pin, tack and stitch.

▪ Place over fireplace and check that it fits neatly. Roll up front and tie tapes together to hold.

transform your home

LITTLE WHITE TIES

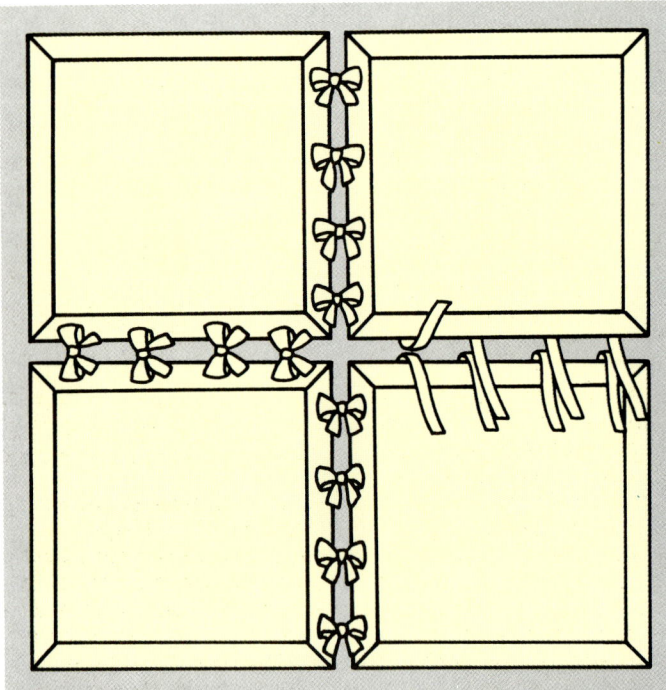

THE TABLECLOTH
▨ From fabric, cut out four 40¼in (102cm) squares. Also cut enough 1¾in (4.2cm) strips of binding to make up 16 lengths, one for each side of each fabric square. Cut 32 lengths of white binding tape, each 12in (30cm) long, for ties.
▨ Position ties on squares, four ties each on two joining edges of each square. Space the ties evenly, with short raw edge of tie matching the raw edge of the fabric, and the tie lying on the wrong side of the fabric. Make sure that all ties match on all four squares, so that the finished squares will join neatly.
▨ Taking a scant ¼in (6mm) seam allowance, stitch ties to fabric.
▨ With right side of binding to wrong side of fabric, and keeping ties lying flat on the fabric, pin, tack and stitch one strip of binding to one side of a fabric square, taking a ¼in (6mm) seam allowance. Begin and end stitching ¼in (6mm) in from each raw side edge. At each corner, fold back the binding at a 45 degree angle and press. Stitch remaining binding strips to edges in the same way.
▨ When all strips have been stitched in place, bring pressed corner lines together and stitch along the folds to make mitered corners. Trim corners, then turn under a ¼in (6mm) seam allowance all around border strips. Bring binding over to right side of fabric and topstitch in position, stitching close to both the inner and outer edges of the binding.
▨ Tie squares together to complete the cloth.

THE PLAIN CHAIR COVER
▨ Each chair is different, so your cover must to some extent be shaped to your particular chair, but there is no need for it to fit closely: the cover is supposed to be loose and just tied together at either side of the chair at the back. It is cut in five pieces: one piece runs from the base at the back, over the top of the chair and down across the seat and on to the base; two arm pieces run up from the base over each arm, meeting the main piece at the side, and two arm fronts join the arms to the main piece at the front of the chair.
▨ Measure the chair for the main piece, from front base to back base and taking the widest measurement to give the width (the piece must be cut wide enough to be brought around the front of the chair to join with the back at the sides). Cut out, adding ⅝in (1.5cm) for each side seam and 1½in (4cm) for each base hem. Cut out all other pieces in the same way.
▨ Lay the main piece on the chair, wrong side out. Bring the front over the sides at the back of the chair and pin at the top.
▨ Trim the back portion to meet the front and the side edges at

the back of the chair. Again with wrong sides out, pin the main arm sections to the main piece, trimming as necessary to get a good fit, but leaving ⅝in (1.5cm) seam allowances, and making sure that arm sections can easily be tied to back down side edges. Fit, pin and trim arm fronts to arms and main section. Mark all seamlines with pins or tailors' chalk, remembering that the fit should be generous rather than tight.
▨ Remove cover and stitch all seams. Finish off outside edges which meet down the back with binding, as for the fireplace cover. Make ties as for the fireplace cover and stitch them down the back edges in matching pairs. Turn up and stitch a double ¾in (2cm) hem at the base of the cover.
▨ Place cover over chair and tie bows across back edges.

LITTLE WHITE TIES

THE BLACK AND WHITE COVERS

▪ The main piece runs from the top of the chair, down the front, across the seat and down to the floor level. Measure the back from top to floor level, and measure for two side pieces which run from the edge of the seat down to floor level and from the front edge to the back edge of the chair.

▪ Cut out all four pieces, adding ⅝in (1.5cm) seam allowances to all joining edges and 1½in (4cm) to the base edge.

▪ Join back to front, then join in the sides. Cut binding strips and bind the side edges at the back of the cover, as for fireplace. Make tapes as for fireplace and stitch in pairs along the bound edges.

▪ Place cover on chair, right side out, and gently mark in a design of your choosing, using a pencil. Remove the cover and work over the design lines, either with a close zigzag stitch or with a fabric painting pen. If you are using a

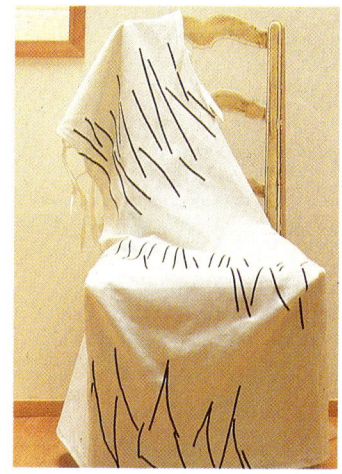

machine zigzag stitch, work from the center of the design outwards, whenever possible, to ease out any puckers and avoid distorting the fabric. For the same reason, you may find that you get better results if you run over the lines twice, with a fairly open stitch.

SCATTERED FLOWERS

If you have an old or antique chair which you would like to recover, here is a charming way to do it with the minimum of effort for the maximum of effect: an easy-to-work needlepoint design which takes full advantage of the attractive, neutral tone and interesting texture of embroidery canvas and uses it as the background to a design of tiny, scattered flower sprays. Instead of spending hours and hours filling in a monotone background, you are left with the pleasant task of working the little flowers – if the idea wasn't so successful it would seem like cheating! The instructions explain how to remove the old covers and replace them with the finished needlepoint, though you may prefer to let a professional fit the new covers if you do not enjoy upholstery and you are afraid of spoiling the finished work.

Size: to the measure of your existing chair cover.

MATERIALS

Double-thread 10-gauge canvas: separate pieces for the front, back and seat of the chair
DMC tapestry wool in the following colors:
white rose – gray 7321, 7333; white; yellow 7431 and 7745; orange 7445; green 7320, 7384
pink rose – yellow 7431, 7786; pink 7200, 7202, 7204; orange 7445; green 7362, 7382, 7542; white
yellow rose – orange 7445; yellow 7726, 7727; green 7369, 7370, 7548, 7584; white
(Quantities are not given as the amount required will vary according to your chair size and the spacing you choose to give between flowers.
Tapestry needle size 18 or 20
Tapestry frame – you could work without one, but a frame would make stitching easier and would help to prevent the canvas from becoming distorted
Cotton fabric (if undercover needs replacing)
3⁄8in (10mm) fine tacks
Two gimp pins
5⁄8in (1.5cm) wide braid
Curved upholstery needle
Matching thread
Fabric adhesive
Note *If the above yarns are unobtainable, refer to page 80.*

DIRECTIONS

▤ Using a wooden mallet and a ripping chisel, remove old back, front and seat covers, easing out old tacks and always working in the direction of the wood grain.
▤ If necessary, add more padding to the underneath and replace or renew undercover.
▤ Measure the seat both ways and buy canvas to this size, plus at least 8in (20cm) all around. Do the same for inside and outside back.

TAPESTRY

▤ To prevent fraying, bind the canvas edges with masking tape or turn under and stitch a narrow hem.
▤ The motifs are all worked in half cross stitch (see page 7) and each square represents one stitch. Embroider the motifs from the charts, using the photograph as a general guide to positioning. The background is unworked.
▤ As each piece is completed, stretch the canvas back into shape by blocking it: remove binding or holding stitches around edge and if there is a selvage cut small nicks along it to ensure the canvas can be stretched. Dampen the canvas with a wet sponge or a laundry spray.
▤ Take a piece of wood or

chair cover

SCATTERED FLOWERS

KEY

A
- 7320
- 7384
- 7333
- 7321
- 7745
- 7431 also B
- white also B and C
- 7445 also B and C

B
- 7542
- 7382
- 7362
- 7786
- 7204
- 7202
- 7200

C
- 7584
- 7548
- 7369
- 7370
- 7726
- 7727

blockboard larger than the finished embroidery, draw the correct outline of the completed embroidery with a waterproof pen and tape it to the board. Starting at the center top and bottom of the surplus canvas, lightly tack the canvas to the board, following the marked paper outline. Repeat at the sides, making sure that the warp and weft threads are at right angles. Hammer in tacks securely, then wet the canvas again and leave to dry slowly at room temperature over several days. Repeat as necessary until canvas is restored to shape.

THE COVERING
▨ Place the canvas over the seat and temporarily tack to front and side rails, stretching it taut. Smooth back edge down between back and seat and tack at back of chair to back rail.
▨ At front corners, pull side canvas around to the front rail and tack. Fold excess canvas at the front into a pleat in line with edge of seat (trimming off any excess canvas inside. Tack in place. Handstitch down the folded fabric at each front corner.
▨ Check that the seat is smooth and taut and hammer in the tacks.
▨ Center front canvas over chair back and temporarily tack to back of frame at top and sides. Pull lower edge through to the back of the chair and temporarily tack in place. At each side of top, excess canvas will have to be pleated up into small evenly spaced darts – make sure you have the same number of darts at each side. When the darts look right, hammer in the tacks.
▨ Cut the cotton fabric to fit outside back; centrally place over the back and tack in place inside previous row of tacks.
▨ Center the canvas over the cotton fabric on outside back, cutting and then turning under the top and side edges, following the lines of the chair and covering over previous tacks; pin in place. Secure lower edge with tacks. Using a curved needle, stitch the side and top edges to the inside back canvas.
▨ Cover tack heads at base with braid. Tack the end in place with a gimp pin, fold braid over tack and glue in place all around the base edge. Secure the opposite end with a gimp pin to finish.

COLOR AND LIGHT

Even in the middle of winter, this needlepoint mat will give you the feeling of warm sunshine pouring in through a stained glass window, illuminating an intricate pattern of bright, jewel-like colors. The dark outlines, like the leading in a window, enhance the colors until they seem to glow with life. Although the pattern is complex, it is worked on a large-scale canvas, which can be covered quickly.

Size: approximately 32in × 52in (80cm × 130cm).

MATERIALS

1 1/8yd × 1 5/8yd (1m × 1.5m) of 4-gauge DMC rug canvas
DMC rug wool (uncut) as follows: seven hanks of gray 7333; four hanks of ecru; two hanks each of primrose 7504, blue 7313 and black, and one hank each of gold 7505, blue 7301, 7305, 7307, 7317 and 7326, pink 7120, 7196, 7202 and 7206, beige 7491, green 7347, sand 7520, bronze 7421 and tan 7446 and 7444
Strong button thread
Large tapestry or rug needle
Fine-tip waterproof felt marker
Note If the above yarn is unobtainable, refer to page 80.

DIRECTIONS

▪ Draw a vertical line with the marker through the center of the canvas, taking care not to cross any vertical threads. Mark the central horizontal line in the same way. Rule the corresponding lines across the chart to find the center of the design.
▪ Bind the edges of the canvas with masking tape to prevent the threads unravelling. Begin stitching at the center of the canvas, working outwards and following the chart square by square. Each square on the chart represents one half cross stitch.
▪ Embroider the stained glass design first, and then work the black and gray border.
▪ Block the embroidery (see page 26) if it has pulled out of shape during stitching, then trim away the surplus canvas, leaving a margin of 2in (5cm) all around the embroidery.
▪ The rug can either be bound with strips of rug binding, as described on page 14, or finished as follows: cutting diagonally across, trim spare canvas from corners to reduce bulk. Fold the canvas to the back at each corner, then bring the side margins to the back to meet at a mitered fold.
▪ Using strong button thread, stitch the sides together along the mitered corners, then secure all edges to the back of the rug with herringbone stitch.

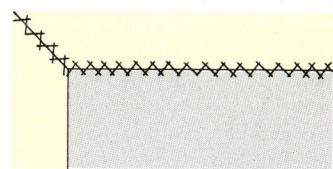

COLOR AND LIGHT

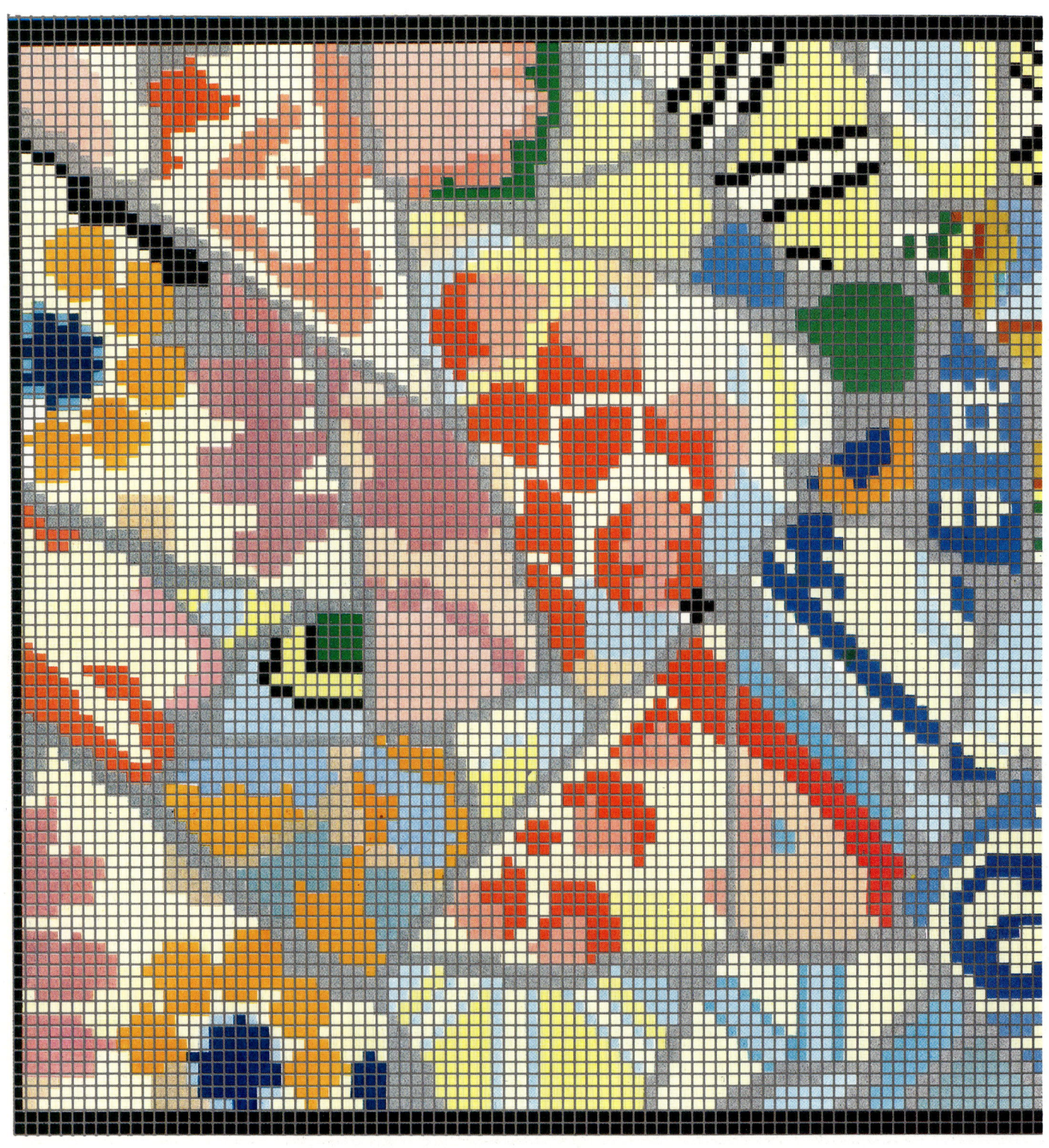

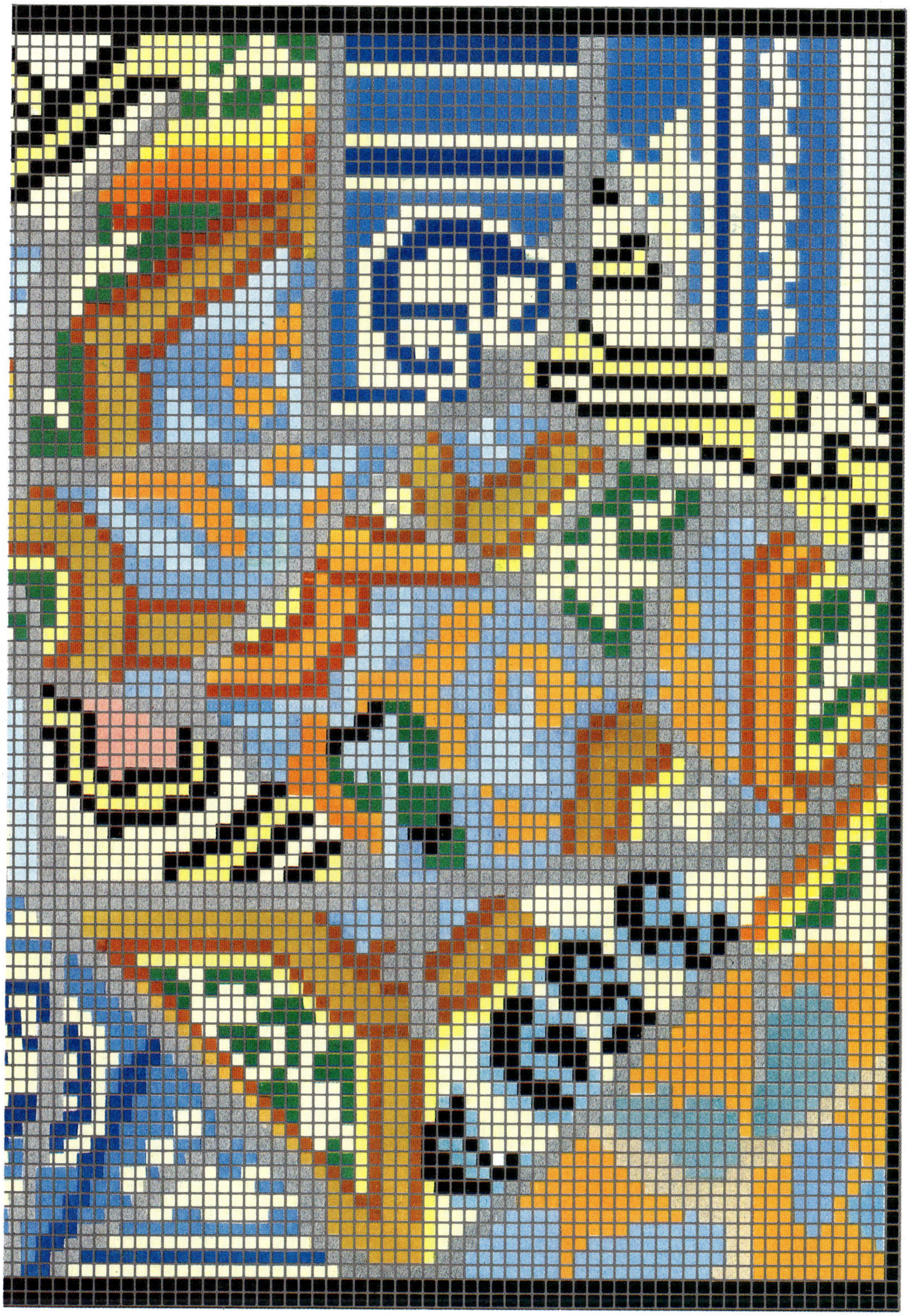

COLOR AND LIGHT

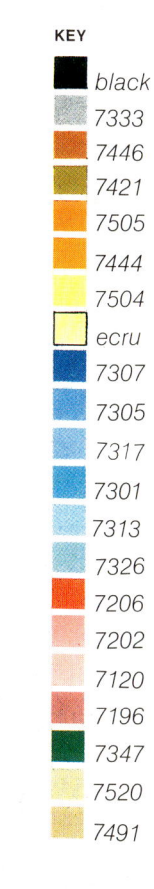

KEY

- ■ black
- 7333
- 7446
- 7421
- 7505
- 7444
- 7504
- ecru
- 7307
- 7305
- 7317
- 7301
- 7313
- 7326
- 7206
- 7202
- 7120
- 7196
- 7347
- 7520
- 7491

The pattern shows the central portion of the mat. In addition, there is an inner border of two rows of stitches in black, running all around the work, and an outer border of gray, seven rows deep. The black inner border emphasizes the bright colors of the design and throws them into sharp relief, while the gray outer border suggests the stone walls which so often surround a stained glass window. If you wish to change the color of the outer border to match your surroundings, either make a tracing of the design and color it in, adding the borders, or shade strips of paper in the chosen border color and frame them around the design.

29

HOLIDAY FUN CURTAIN

This bright, cheerful door curtain, an effective screen between a cool interior and the blazing sun outside, is made by threading colorful strips of bias binding through the open mesh of the net. It's so easy that even a child could do it, instantly turning a utilitarian screen into something festive and informal, happily at home with cottage flowers and sunny summer days.

Size: made to fit your door or window space.

MATERIALS

Heavy cotton netting with an open mesh (the holes should be distributed in a regular pattern and large enough to hold the folded tape easily)
1in (2.5cm) wide bias binding in green, yellow, red, pink, violet, blue and black (market stalls are often a cheap source)
4in (10cm) wide white fringe for lower edge
Bodkin for threading
Matching thread

DIRECTIONS

▪ Measure the door or window opening and cut fabric to this size, adding 4in (10cm) to the width for side hem allowances plus ease, and a sufficient allowance to the length for the desired finish at the top edge.
▪ Turn under a double ⅝in (1.5cm) hem down both side edges; pin, tack and stitch.
▪ Turn up lower edge of curtain to right side for ⅜in (1cm); pin and tack. Position fringe over turned-up edge, turning in the outer edges, in line with side hems. Pin, tack and topstitch fringe in place.
▪ Finish the top edge of the curtain in the desired way.
▪ Using pins, mark the position of the design, about one design width from lower edge. The spacing will depend to some extent on the length of the curtain, but it would be better to have more plain curtain above the design than below.
▪ Thread a manageable length – about 16in (40cm) – of binding through the bodkin, folding the binding in half widthwise, with raw edges inside. Following the diagram for colors and pattern, weave the bodkin in and out through the natural gaps in the fabric. Cut the binding at the end of each line of the design, leaving loose ends of equal length – about ⅜in (1cm) at either end.

Note The curtain can either be finished at the top with ordinary curtain tape (which would then be left ungathered) and hung from a curtain rail or pole, or you could make a casing at the top and thread this over a dowel or pole.

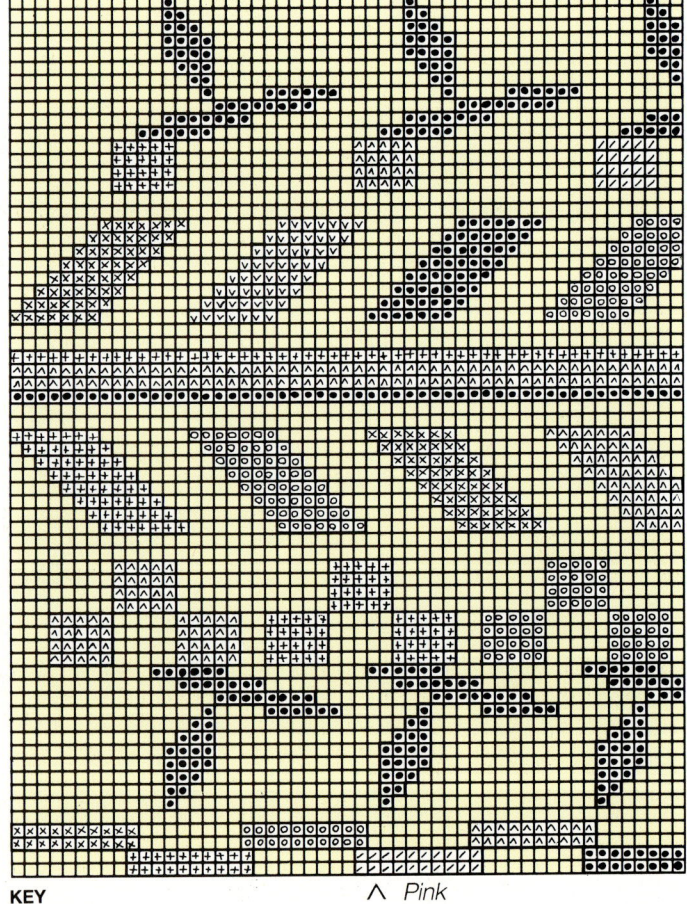

KEY
● Green
○ Yellow
× Red
∧ Pink
∨ Violet
+ Blue
/ Black

simply child's play

INSTANT SEATING

The elegant contrast between sober navy and pure white gives these simple box cushions an air of great style, but they are also extremely comfortable, with two layers of foam, one on top of the other. Use them for sitting or just for lounging about, tucking them away in a corner when you don't need them, and when you want to wash the white covers you simply untie the knots and lift them off.

Size: 12in (30cm) high and 26in (65cm) square.

MATERIALS

Two 26in × 26in (65cm × 65cm) blocks of 6in (15cm) deep foam
1⅜yd (1.2m) of 56in (140cm) wide white woven fabric
1⅞yd (1.7m) of 45in (115cm) wide navy woven fabric
13¾yd (12.5m) or 10¼yd (9.3m) of 1in (2.5cm) wide navy tape (amount varies according to whether tape is stitched in double or single lines)
Matching threads

DIRECTIONS

▢ For the base cushion, cut two pieces each 27¼in × 27¼in (68cm × 68cm) from navy fabric, and four side gusset pieces, each 27¼in × 7¼in (68cm × 18cm).

▢ The tapes on the top cover are formed either in two double lines running each way or with three evenly spaced strands running each way. Cut 6¾in (17cm) lengths of tape and stitch them to side gusset pieces of base to correspond with chosen pattern for top: either four or three for each side, and positioned 3½in (9cm) up from the lower edge.

▢ Taking ⅝in (1.5cm) seam allowances, pin, tack and stitch gusset pieces into a ring, beginning and ending stitching ⅝in (1.5cm) from ends of each seam.

▢ Pin, tack and stitch gusset to base cushion piece, matching seams to corners. Pin, tack and stitch top cushion piece to opposite edge of gusset in the same way, but leaving an opening on one side and the first 3in (7.5cm) of the adjoining sides. Trim and turn cover to the right side. Insert foam; turn in the raw edges in line with the remainder of the seam and slipstitch together to close.

▢ For top cover, cut 48in × 48in (120cm × 120cm) of white fabric. Center the fabric over the second foam block and mark the corners with pins.

▢ Position strips of tape across the fabric, either with two double lines running each way or with three evenly spaced strands running each way. Place second block over first and fabric over both to check that top tapes will join neatly and accurately with bottom tapes. The strips should be 3½in (8.5cm) longer than the fabric at either end. Pin and stitch the tapes in position, stitching close to the edge down each side and stopping 2½in (6.5cm) short of the raw edge of the fabric at either end, leaving 6in (15cm) free to form ties.

▢ Make a ¾in (2cm) wide buttonhole in the cover ½in (13mm) below the stitching at the end of each tape.

▢ Stack uncovered foam block on top of covered foam, matching edges. Place fabric, wrong side out, centered over the foam blocks and pin darts at each corner so that the cover fits smoothly over the blocks. Work from top corners downwards and leave darts unpinned for the last 2½in (6.5cm) from base edge.

▢ Remove cover; pin, tack and stitch darts up to 2½in (6.5cm)

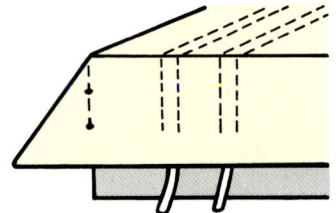

from base edge.

▢ Press darts, including unstitched ends. Cut along foldline, and press darts open. Finish raw edges and slipstitch allowances neatly in place at the back of the cover.

▢ Turn up a 1½in (4cm) hem around lower edge of top cover and stitch.

▢ Replace cover on blocks; thread lower tapes through buttonholes and tie them to the upper tapes.

comfort with style

GEOMETRIC PERFECTION

Dark blue embroidery on pure white cotton piqué makes an elegant and unusual floor covering, visually interesting yet at the same time in perfect harmony with the cool, uncluttered modern style. White cotton might seem impractical as a floor covering – and indeed you could equally well use this as a wall hanging or a bed throw – but it is machine washable. If you have time to spare, you could even embroider a kimono to match.

Size: 52in × 52in (130cm × 130cm).

MATERIALS

3yd (2.7m) of 54in (135cm) wide white cotton piqué
3yd (2.7m) of 36in (90cm) wide lightweight polyester padding
DMC coton à broder: 35 skeins of blue 2336
Tracing paper
Dressmakers' carbon paper
Matching thread

DIRECTIONS

▨ Cut two pieces of cotton piqué, each measuring 53½in × 53½in (133cm × 133cm). Also cut two lengths of padding, each 52in (130cm) long
▨ Place the strips of padding side by side and herringbone stitch the edges together. Turn the pieces the other way up and repeat the process. Trim the resulting piece of padding to measure 52in × 52in (130cm × 130cm).
▨ Draw a grid on tracing paper and scale up the design. Position the tracing paper over the center of one fabric square, on the right side of the fabric, and pin both fabric and paper to a flat surface, pinning around the edge of the design. Slide the carbon paper, coated side down, between the fabric and the paper design. Because of the scale of the design, you may find it necessary to work section by section. Trace over the design, marking it on the fabric.
▨ Leaving an even ⅝in (1.5cm) margin of cotton piqué all around, pin and tack the polyester padding to the wrong side of the marked cotton. Place the padded and unpadded cotton squares with right sides together and pin, tack and stitch together around the outer edge, taking a ⅝in (1.5cm) seam allowance and leaving a gap for turning.
▨ Turn the square right side out, enclosing the padding. Fold in seam allowances along the gap and slipstitch to close.
▨ Smooth out the three layers and make lines of tacking across the fabric, vertically and horizontally, at intervals of about 4in (10cm), taking care not to ruckle the layers.
▨ Using three strands of embroidery cotton in your needle, embroider the design. The dots marked A consist of a cluster of seven French knots, as shown on page 36. The section of the design marked B is worked in a graduated satin stitch. It is not essential that all stitches should pass through all three layers, but the layers should be held together at intervals of approximately 4in (10cm), or the finished mat may tend to ruckle.
▨ When the central design is complete, topstitch all around the mat in matching thread, ¾in (2cm) from the outer edge.
▨ Using three strands of embroidery cotton, complete the design with diagonal lines of large darning stitches across the undecorated section, stitching through all layers and finishing off neatly.

cool summer mat

GEOMETRIC PERFECTION

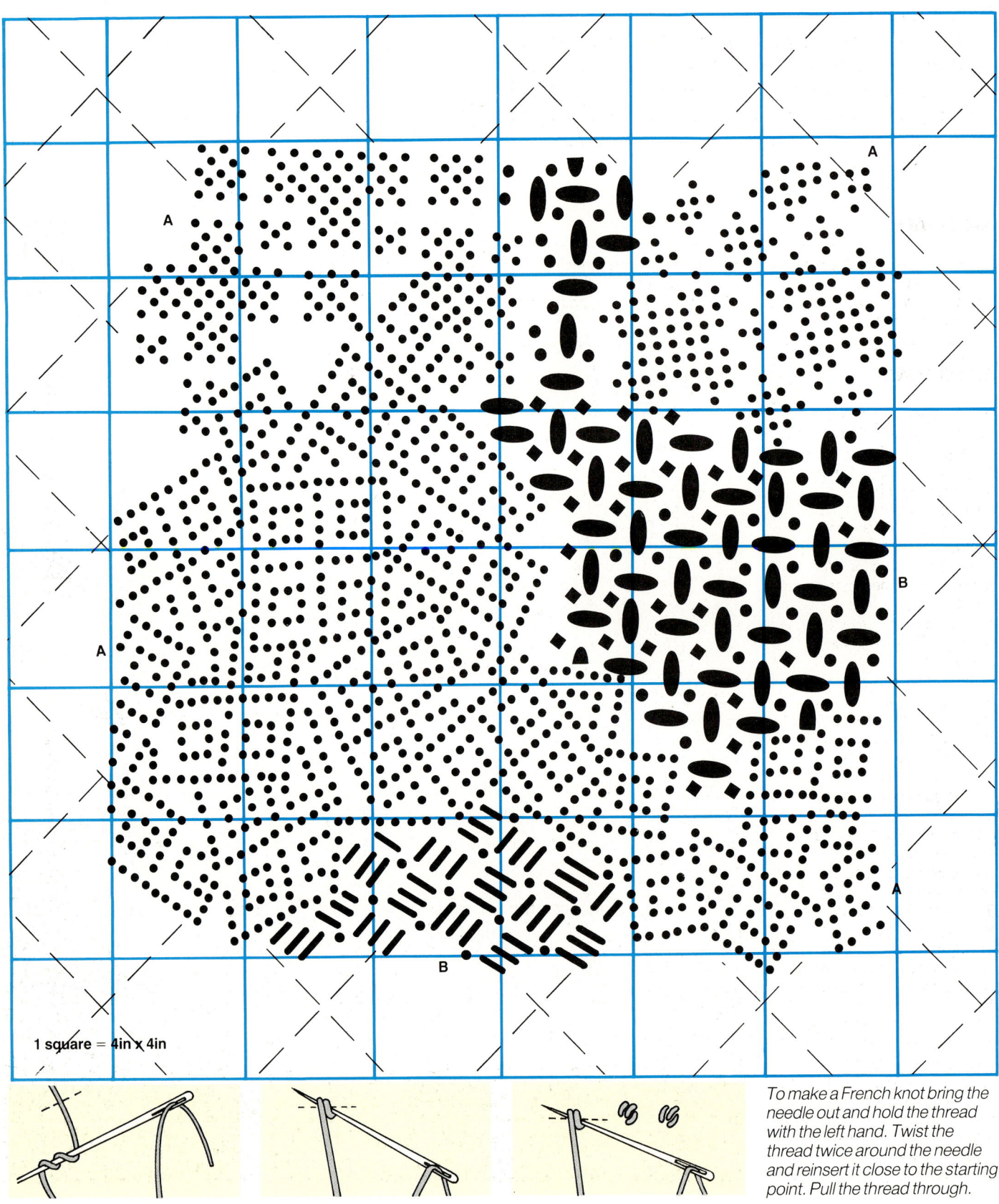

1 square = 4in x 4in

To make a French knot bring the needle out and hold the thread with the left hand. Twist the thread twice around the needle and reinsert it close to the starting point. Pull the thread through.

PRISMATIC NET

Let the sun filter into your room through a fine net curtain decorated with bright triangles set at random, sending patches of multi-colored light dancing over your walls and floor. This unusual and amusing idea is very quick to make, but it gives you plenty of scope to indulge your creative side.

Size: to fit your window.

MATERIALS

White or light-colored net fabric (see below for quantity)
Odds and ends of net fabric in a range of colors
Eyelets and eyelet punch
Matching thread
¾in (2cm) diameter curtain pole plus fixing brackets

DIRECTIONS

▪ Measure the window and cut out one piece of net fabric to this length plus 11in (28cm) for hem and casing and to one-and-a-half times the finished width. If necessary to gain the curtain width, cut out two or more lengths and stitch together with flat fell seams to achieve the correct size. Remember when calculating the width to measure across the full desired width, not just the inside width of the window frame.
▪ Turn under a double ¾in (2cm) hem on both side edges and pin. Turn under a double 2in (5cm) hem along base edge and pin. Miter the bottom corners. Tack and stitch all hems.
▪ At the top, turn under a double 3½in (9cm) hem/casing. Pin, tack and stitch across, close to the folded lower edge. Stitch across hem/casing again, just below top edge.
▪ Make a card template of an equilateral triangle with 4in (10cm) sides. Using template and colored pencils, mark triangles on net odds and ends and cut out.
▪ Lay the curtain right side up on the floor or other large flat surface. Selecting points at random, pin two or three triangles at a time to the curtain, moving triangles so that they do not lie directly on top of each other. Fix each group with an eyelet.
▪ Hang the curtain on the pole.

A ROSE IS A ROSE

Turn an uninteresting view into something with a hint of magic and suspense with this light, airy blind. The secret lies in the clear plastic window set into white satin; for windows within windows, like boxes within boxes, convey a feeling of mystery and the excitement of discovery. In this case, the window has its own hidden secret, for the decoration of corded scrollwork with which it is covered is not a random tangle, as might at first appear, but the word 'rose', repeated over and over again.

Size: this can be adjusted to individual requirements; the central plastic window measures 7in × 6in (17.5cm × 15cm).

MATERIALS

White satin – to your measurements (see below)
7¾in × 6¾in (19.5cm × 17cm) sheet of transparent plastic
4½yd (4m) of flat white cord
Fabric adhesive
Matching thread
Length of 1in (2.5cm) diameter dowel to fit across window, plus fixing brackets

DIRECTIONS

▦ Measure the window and cut out satin to this size, adding 5½in (14cm) to the length for top casing and base hem and 1½in (4cm) to the width for side hems.
▦ Turn under double ⅜in (1cm) wide hem down both side edges and along base edge, forming neat base corners. Pin, tack and stitch hems in place.
▦ For top casing turn under ⅜in (1cm), then a further 4⅜in (11cm); pin, tack and stitch across blind.
▦ Starch and iron the satin. Mark the center lengthwise.
▦ Mark, with tacking stitches, a 7in × 6in (17.5cm × 15cm) window centered on blind, about two thirds up from base edge. Cut out a central section 6¼in × 5¼in (15.5cm × 13cm) from inside the marked rectangle and discard. Snip into the corners up to the tacking stitches; turn back the edges along the tacked lines, and carefully glue them to the wrong side, removing the tacking stitches as you work.
▦ Following the design, glue the cord over one side of the plastic sheet in loops, being careful not to spread adhesive on the clear plastic areas. Leave to dry.
▦ Center the plastic design behind the window and glue in place to turned-back edges of fabric. If necessary, topstitch around edge of window.
▦ Slide dowel through top casing and hang blind.

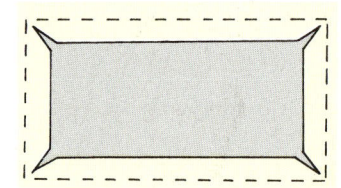

blind with a view

BUTTERFLY PICNIC

A host of butterflies with dazzling wings dances around a damask tablecloth, spilling over onto the napkins – what better setting could you provide for an elegant outdoor feast on a summer's day? Perhaps a few real butterflies will be lured into joining you if you are really lucky. The damask background provides a subtle extra dimension against which you can display as many or as few butterflies as you wish, depending on your personal taste and how energetic you are feeling.

Size: tablecloth 45in × 54in (115cm × 135cm); napkin 16in × 16in (40cm × 40cm). The quanties given are for the tablecloth in the photograph but you can easily make yours smaller or larger.

MATERIALS

2¼yd (2m) of 56in (140cm) wide cotton or linen damask – sufficient for one tablecloth and up to six napkins
DMC stranded cotton, one skein each of the following colours: brown 300 and 976, black 310, gray 413, yellow 444, 676 and 742, orange 972 and 973, blue 792, 799 and 800, turquoise 995 and 996, lilac 553, green 701, 907, 943, 991 and 993, and white
15½yd (14m) of ½in (13mm) wide blue satin bias binding (for tablecloth and six napkins)
Crewel needle size 6 or 7
Tracing paper
Dressmakers' carbon paper
Matching sewing thread
Note If the above yarn is unobtainable, refer to page 80.

DIRECTIONS

▪ Using a pencil mark one rectangle 45in × 54in (115cm × 135cm) for the tablecloth and six 16in (40cm) squares for the napkins on the damask. Cut out, allowing a small margin of spare fabric around each for fraying.
▪ Enlarge the butterfly motifs onto tracing paper and transfer them to the cloth, using the photograph as a general guide to positioning, but choosing for yourself how many motifs you wish to repeat and where.
▪ Using three strands of thread throughout and keeping the fabric stretched in the embroidery hoop, embroider the motifs. Embroider the butterflies in satin stitch, using the photograph as a stitch guide.
▪ For each napkin, work one or two butterflies in one corner.
▪ When the embroidered pieces are completed, place them face downwards on a well-padded surface and press them lightly.
▪ Trim all pieces back to the marked pencil line. For each napkin, take a 66in (165cm) length of binding. Turn ¼in (6mm) under at one short end and with the binding out flat and matching the folded end to the edge at one side of the napkin, lay the binding along one side, with the edge of the binding a scant ¼in (6mm) in from the raw edge of the napkin. Pin and tack. At the corner adjust the binding so that it will run easily around the corner when brought over to cover the edge. Work around the napkin in this manner. At the final corner, turn under the short raw edge of the binding for ¼in (6mm), folding it at a mitered angle and trimming away any excess length. Make sure that it will completely cover the other end.
▪ Stitch the binding to napkin, bring it over to the wrong side, making mitered folds at the corners, and pin and slipstich by hand to the other side. (For a more hand-finished effect, machine the binding to the wrong side first and then slipstitch to the right side.)
▪ Complete the tablecloth in the same manner.

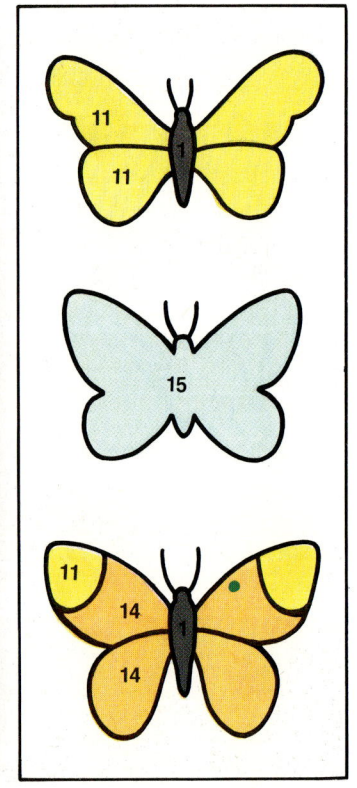

embroidered damask

BUTTERFLY PICNIC

BUTTERFLY PICNIC

KEY

1	413
2	799
3	792
4	976
5	972
6	996
7	300
8	676
9	553
10	973
11	444
12	943
13	701
14	742
15	800
16	995
17	310
18	907
19	991
20	993
21	white

43

BOUND WITH BOWS

An attractive tablemat and matching napkin help to set the scene for a celebration, giving your table an appropriately light and festive air, whatever the occasion. Choose bright red or green for Christmas or pretty pastels for a summer tea party; pick a contrast fabric which will harmonize with curtains or other elements of your decor, or make a harlequin set with a different color for every member of the family.

Sizes: tablemat approximately 19½in × 11½in (49cm × 29cm); napkin 15¼in (38cm) square.

MATERIALS

Quantities are for one mat and one napkin:
⅝yd (50cm) of 36in (90cm) wide plain white cotton
8in (20cm) of 36in (90cm) wide contrast fabric

Bonding fabric
Tracing paper
Dressmakers' pattern paper
Matching embroidery cotton
Matching thread

DIRECTIONS

FOR THE TABLEMAT

■ Cut a piece of squared paper 20in × 12in (50cm × 30cm). Fold it carefully in half both ways (into four) and press folds. Draw up the diagram onto one side of the folded paper, with the straight edges running along the folded paper edges. Keeping the paper folded, cut along the shaped outer edge. Unfold the pattern.

■ Using the pattern, cut out one placemat from white cotton – a seam allowance of ¼in (6mm) all around is included.

■ Now draw in the border on the pattern, making it 1½in (3.5cm) wide all around (this includes seam allowances). Using tracing paper, make patterns for the border – one for the sides and one for the top and bottom, angling the corners so that the strips will join at a mitered angle and adding ¼in (6mm) seam allowances at ends.

■ Cut two sides and two top/bottom strips from contrast fabric and join to make a continuous border frame. Turn in and tack a ¼in (6mm) allowance around the inner edge, clipping up to the fold where necessary.

■ With right side of border to wrong side of mat, pin, tack and stitch border to mat, taking a ¼in (6mm) seam allowance all around. Taking notches out of seam allowance where necessary, bring border to right side of mat. Topstitch by machine or blanket stitch by hand to hold border in place around inner edge.

■ Scale up and trace off bow pattern, once with and once without ribbon ends. Mark both shapes on bonding fabric and cut out roughly, allowing a little extra all around. Iron bonding to wrong side of contrast fabric and cut out both shapes.

■ Pull back from bow with ends and position at top right corner of mat. Press in place, then blanket stitch around the outer edge and the knot, anchoring the bow. Add crease lines in stem stitch and scattered dots in satin stitch.

■ Remove backing from bow without ends and iron to wrong side of contrast fabric, then cut out. Blanket stitch around inner lines and knot of contrast bow, adding crease lines in stem stitch as before. Position prepared bow upside down at left-hand corner. Blanket stitch in place, sewing all around the outer edge but only attaching the bow to the mat at either end, leaving the central portion free, to hold the napkin.

FOR THE NAPKIN

■ Cut out one piece of white cotton 15¼in (38cm) square. Bind the napkin in the same way as the place mat, but cutting strips ⅞in (2.2cm) wide, to make a finished border ⅜in (1cm) wide.

■ Trace a bow shape and cut from contrast fabric. Iron to bonding fabric, remove backing, and then iron and blanket stitch to napkin, adding stem stitch and satin stitch details as before.

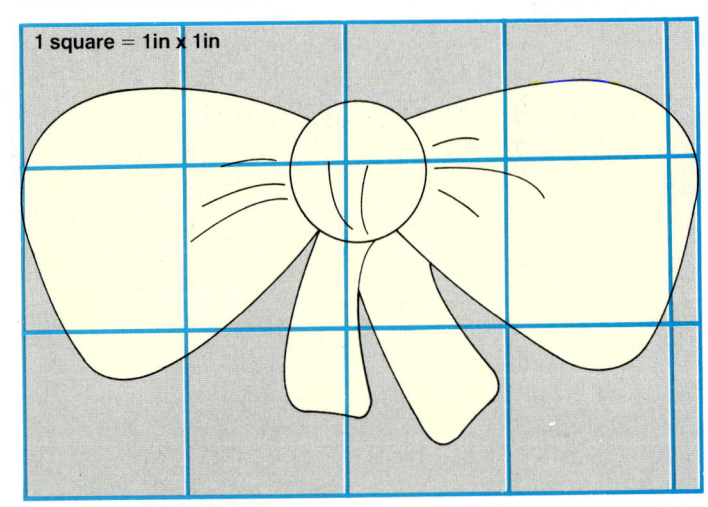

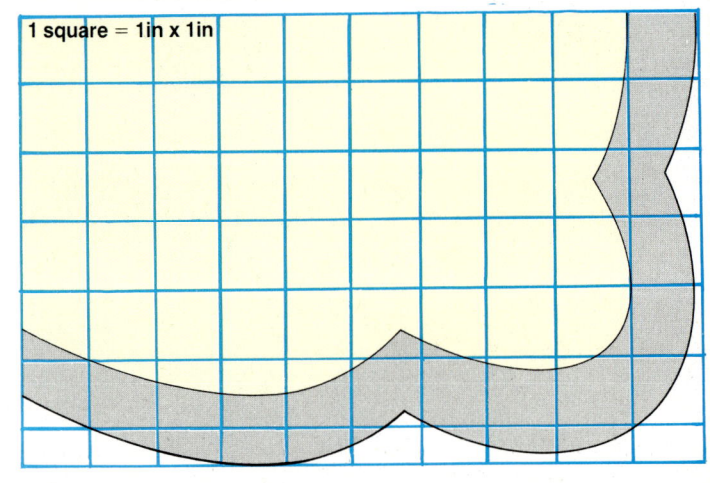

1 square = 1in x 1in

1 square = 1in x 1in

pretty table set

PROVENÇAL PICNIC SET

As soon as warm weather approaches, you can prepare to expand your lifestyle to include elegant outdoor meals and picnics, adding a touch of sophistication with this pretty bordered tablecloth and matching picnic bag. They are very easy to make: the cloth just has a simple border in a contrast fabric; the bag is padded and then lined with a contrast fabric, the patchwork effect coming from the handles which run down the bag to meet at the base. The skill lies in choosing a subtle contrast of fabrics suited to good food and an easy life under the shade of the trees.

Sizes: tablecloth 55½in × 55½in (141cm × 141cm); bag approximately 17½in × 19½in (45cm × 52cm).

MATERIALS

FOR THE TABLECLOTH
1½yd (1.3m) of 50in (128cm) wide printed cotton fabric
1¾yd (1.5m) of 50in (128cm) wide printed cotton fabric in a contrast design
Matching thread

FOR THE BAG
¾yd (60cm) of 50in (128cm) wide printed cotton fabric
1yd (1m) of 50in (128cm) wide printed cotton fabric in a contrast design
1yd (1m) of 36in (90cm) wide lightweight padding
Matching thread

DIRECTIONS

THE TABLECLOTH
▪ From the main fabric cut one piece 48in (122cm) square. For the border, cut four contrast pieces each 56¾in × 9in (144cm × 23cm).
▪ Fold each border strip in half lengthwise. At the corners, bring the short raw edges up to meet along the folded edge and press. Unfold and cut along the pressed lines (see page 7).
▪ Stitching in line with the mitered points, and with wrong sides together, join the strips into a circle, taking ⅝in (1.5cm) seams and stopping ⅜in (1cm) short of the long sides of the strips. Trim and refold strips with right sides out.
▪ Turn in edges of border for ⅜in (1cm) on both sides of strip and press. Place border around central square, so that edges of border overlap the edges of the square for ⅜in (1cm). Pin, tack and topstitch in place.
▪ Work a close zigzag stitch to cover the border joining.

THE BAG
▪ From main fabric cut out one piece 37¾in × 22¾in (96cm × 58cm) for bag. Repeat to cut out one piece the same size from padding and one from contrast fabric.
▪ For handles, from contrast fabric cut four lengths each 35½in × 4in (90cm × 10cm). Place short ends of two handle pieces with right sides together; pin, tack and stitch, taking ⅜in (1cm) seam allowance to form a handle 70¼in × 4in (188cm × 10cm). Repeat for second handle. Press seams open.
▪ Fold one handle in half lengthwise with right sides together. Pin, tack and stitch long edge taking ⅜in (1cm) seam allowance and leaving an opening centered in one side. Trim and turn to right side. Turn in opening edges in line with the remainder of the seam and slipstitch together to close. Press, then zigzag stitch raw ends to close and finish. Repeat, to make up the second handle in the same way.
▪ Place the padding on the wrong side of the main fabric piece; pin and tack together all around. Lay the main fabric piece right side up on a flat surface and position a handle on each side so that the ends of the handles meet at the center of the piece. The two ends of each handle should be positioned parallel to each other and to the side edges of the bag and should lie 5½in (14cm) in from the side edges. Each handle should form a loop projecting beyond the raw edge of the bag. Pin, tack and topstitch the handles in place, stitching to within ⅜in (1cm) of the top edge.
▪ Fold the bag in half widthways with right sides together; pin, tack and stitch sides, taking a ⅜in (1cm) seam allowance. Trim padding right back to seamline and turn bag right side out. Turn up base points of bag to side seam, forming a 1½in (4cm) triangle. Pin and tack, then topstitch down both sides of each side seam, catching in triangle at base.
▪ Fold bag lining in half widthways with right sides together; pin, tack and stitch sides, taking ⅜in (1cm) seam allowance and leaving a center opening in one side large enough to turn bag through at a later stage. Fold up ends as for outer cover, but forming the triangles on the wrong side and catch-stitching them in place.
▪ Place lining over bag with right sides together. Pin, tack and stitch all around top edge, taking ⅜in (1cm) seam allowance. Trim padding right back to seamline and turn bag to right side. Turn in opening edges of lining in line with the remainder of the seam and slipstitch to close. Push lining down inside bag and, if necessary, catch to main fabric and padding at base corners.

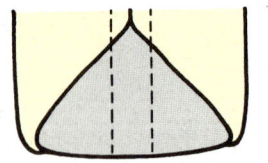

outdoor elegance

LIGHT AS AIR

Fine white organdy, tucked into pleats or shaped into delicate border detailing makes the perfect complement to a glass table set with crystal and fine porcelain – guaranteed to make your soufflés, mousses and meringues a touch lighter! There are three different placemats to choose from: one is flanked by tucks at either side; one has a doubled border shaped into scallops and the third has a plain double-thickness border. The napkin has a simple border of pintucks running right around.

Size: each placemat measures approximately 19in×14¼in (48cm×36cm); napkin 10in×10in (25cm×25cm).

MATERIALS

¾yd (70cm) of 45in (115cm) wide organdy for any one placemat and napkin	Paper – for scalloped edge mat only Matching thread

DIRECTIONS

THE PLEATED MAT

▨ Cut a strip of organdy 33in×15¼in (82cm×38cm). Turn under a double ¼in (6mm) hem along both long edges; pin and tack. Zigzag stitch along both short edges.

▨ Fold fabric in half, bringing short edges together to find vertical center of mat. Mark center point at top and lower edges with pins. Measure out 5in (12.5cm) either way to find point A, stitching line of first tuck.

▨ With wrong sides together, fold fabric to make first tuck, 1⁵⁄₁₆in (3.2cm) deep, with the fold 6⁵⁄₁₆in (15.7cm) from the marked center. Stitch the tuck with ordinary straight stitch. Refold the fabric to make the second tuck, 1¼in (3cm) deep, so that the stitching of the second fold will be just covered by the edge of the first tuck. Stitch, then turn back the last 2in (5cm) and stitch, to make the outer tuck. Make tucks on both sides in this way, with tucks facing outwards.

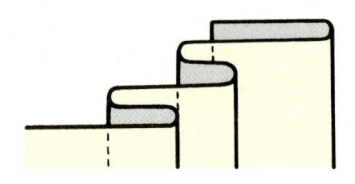

▨ To complete mat, topstitch along both top edges, holding tucks in position, and cover the stitching line of the inner tuck at either side with zigzag stitch or a machine embroidery stitch.

THE SCALLOPED EDGE MAT

▨ Take a piece of paper 19in×14¼in (48cm×36cm). Fold it in half and then in quarters. Using the base of a wine glass, mark scallops along the cut edges: one scallop should run around the corner and another scallop should run at either side from the first scallop up to the folded edge. Cut along the scallops and unfold the paper.

▨ Use this paper pattern to cut out two scalloped rectangles from fabric, adding a ¼in (6mm) seam allowance all around each. On one piece, mark a centered rectangle, 13½in×8in (34cm×20cm) on the fabric.

▨ Place the two pieces of fabric wrong sides together and stitch all around scalloped edge, taking ¼in (6mm) seam allowance. Cut out one side of the fabric only along the marked inner edge and turn the border right side out. Turn in a ¼in (6mm) single hem along the inner rectangular edge, clipping up to the corners if necessary to get a smooth edge. Stitch inner edge in position, either with straight topstitching or with a close zigzag stitch.

THE PLAIN BORDER MAT

▨ Make in the same way as the scalloped edge mat, but without shaping the edges. If desired, decorate the inner and outer edges with satin stitch or other machine embroidery stitching.

THE NAPKIN

▨ From fabric cut out a 12¼in (30.5cm) square. Pin and tack a double ¼in (6mm) hem all around napkin. Finish the edge with a row of machine embroidery or close zigzag stitch to hold and at the same time decorate the edge.

▨ Work a series of three ⅛in (3mm) deep pin tucks, spaced about 1in (2.5cm) apart, along each side of the napkin.

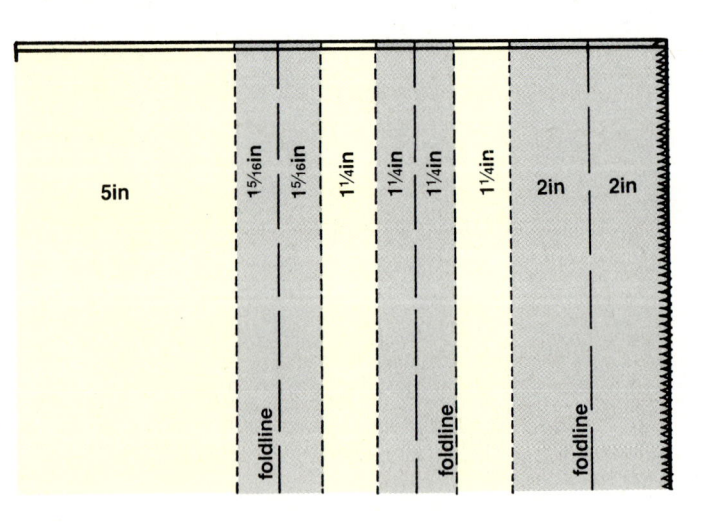

48

organdy placemats and napkins

WHITE AS SNOW

Designed for a gleaming Scandinavian home, all white from cellar to attic, this unusual and elegant cover is decorated with interlaced bands of white leather which provide a subtle and sophisticated contrast with the cellular warmth and soft texture of the background. Use the blanket as a lightweight summer cover or snuggle under it for extra warmth in winter as you drink your ice-cold aquavit.

Size: 55in × 55in (140cm × 140cm).

MATERIALS

1½yd (1.4m) of 55in (140cm) wide cellular blanket fabric *or* an old single blanket or two or more cot blankets joined *or* 25 knitted or crocheted squares each measuring 11in × 11in (28cm × 28cm), joined together to make one large square
Two white lambskins (sufficient to make up strips as listed below) *or* ⅝yd (50cm) of 55in (140cm) wide leather-type fabric
Matching thread

DIRECTIONS

▢ If you are making up the 55in (140cm) square from smaller 11in (28cm) squares, first make the squares, knitting or crocheting them, or cutting up blanketing to size. Finish the edges with zigzag stitch, then lay the pieces side by side and herringbone stitch across the joinings. Join on one side first; turn the work over and join the pieces on the other side. Press lightly.

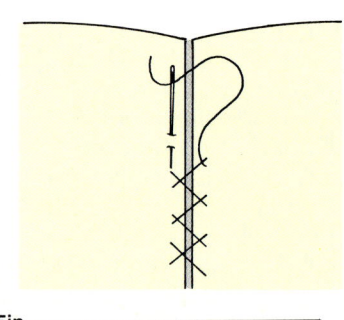

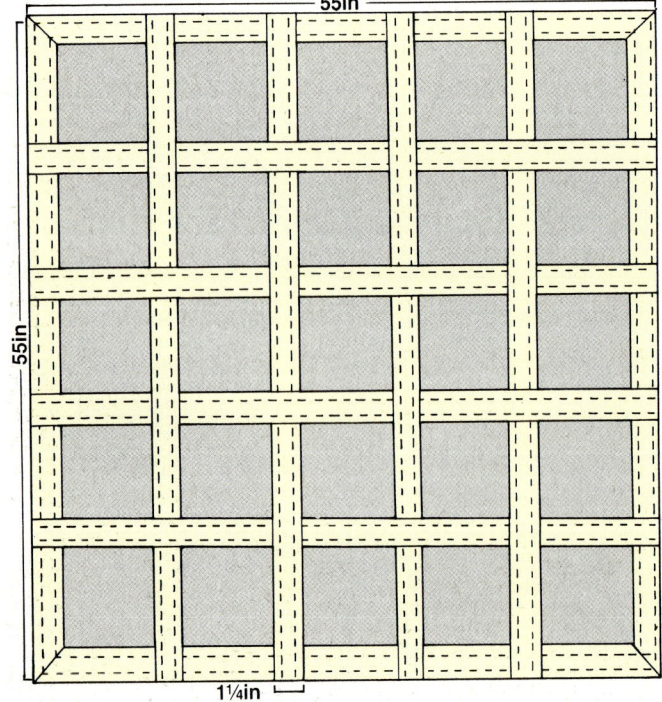

▢ Cut leather into strips as follows, joining pieces as necessary to achieve the correct length: one strip 220in × 2½in (560cm × 6cm) and eight strips 57⅛in × 1¼in (146cm × 3cm).

▢ Fold the long strip in half lengthwise, with right sides together, and place it over the edge of the blanket, with the edge of the blanket against the inner fold edge of the strip. Hold in place with paper clips. Fold each corner into a miter and position the ends of the strip so that they will be covered by one of the strips laid across the blanket.

▢ Remove strip from blanket and stitch corner miters. Trim and press seams open, then turn strip right side out and once again clip around edge of blanket. Topstitch in position, close to the edges of the leather.

▢ Lay the blanket flat and position four 1½in (3cm) wide strips across it at intervals of 11in (28cm), covering the joined edges of any squares (if necessary). The 1¼in (3cm) extra length at each end is brought around to the back of the blanket. Lay the remaining four strips across, interweaving them with the first as shown in the diagram. The strips are topstitched to the blanket down both edges, so place any essential pins along the future lines of stitching, to avoid marking the leather.

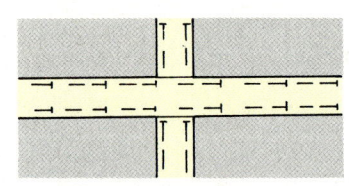

▢ The strips must be sewn in position one by one. Note where subsequent strips will lie over the strip which is being sewn and hold these strips clear of the stitching, pinning them back in position after the stitching is complete, so that the finished lines of stitching follow the interwoven pattern.

for Scandinavian warmth

BEDROOM PAGEANTRY

There is more than a hint of medieval pomp and pageantry in this room, transformed from a straightforward bedroom into a royal tent by the simple addition of tabbed curtains, a luxuriously swathed and tied canopy and an unusual, envelope-like duvet cover with matching pillowcases. Great fun for anyone with a taste for the dramatic, this lavish and splendid effect is not in the least difficult to achieve.

Sizes: curtains and canopy to your required measurements; duvet cover 80in×80in (200cm×200cm); pillowcases 31½in×20in (79cm×50cm).

MATERIALS

CANOPY
Fabric – see below for quantity; the fabric should preferably have no very marked right and wrong sides
Matching thread
Two lengths of ⅝in (1.5cm) dowel, the width of the bed plus 8in (20cm), and cords and hooks for hanging
Length of 2in × ¾in (5cm × 2cm) batten, the width of the bed
Screws to fix batten
Fabric adhesive or staples

FOR THE CURTAINS
Fabric – see below for quantity
Contrast fabric – small amount for curtain loops
2in (5cm) strip of iron-on interfacing the width of the curtain
1½in (3.5cm) diameter buttons – two for each tab required
Matching thread
Dowel pole for hanging
Brackets to fix dowel to window frame

FOR THE DUVET COVER AND PILLOWCASES
4⅝yd (4.1m) of 90in (228cm) wide sheeting
3yd (2.6m) of 90in (228cm) wide sheeting in a contrast pattern
Twenty-eight 1½in (3.5cm) diameter buttons
Matching thread

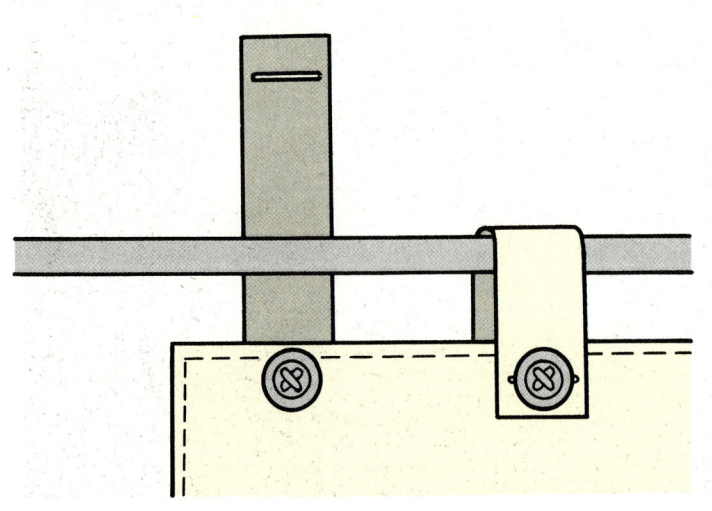

DIRECTIONS

THE CANOPY
▪ Fix hooks in ceiling and hang dowels about 88in (220cm) above the floor, one at the head and one at the foot of the bed. The batten will be screwed to the wall about 30in (75cm) above the headboard.
▪ To measure for fabric, pin a length of string to the wall at batten height and take the string over the dowels and down to the floor, allowing for generous loops of fabric and sufficient at the foot of the bed to tie a loose knot and drape the remainder on the floor. For the width, allow one-and-half times the length of the batten.
▪ Cut out fabric, joining lengths if necessary to achieve the width with flat fell seams. Either leave selvages or turn under a double ⅜in (1cm) hem down both long edges; pin, tack and stitch. Turn under a ⅜in (1cm) hem along base edge; pin, tack and stitch.
▪ Work two rows of gathering stitches along remaining short edge and pull up to fit batten, then fasten off.
▪ Paint the batten the same color as the wall. When dry, fix the raw gathered edge of fabric to the 2in (5cm) side which will be against the wall. With fabric hanging down, fix batten to wall.
▪ Bring fabric up over both lengths of dowel; tie into a single knot and arrange in folds at floor level.

THE CURTAINS
▪ For each curtain required, fix dowel pole in position across window. Measure from dowel to chosen length and add 7in (17.5cm). Curtain width is one-and-a-quarter times the length of the dowel (this includes allowance for side hems).
▪ Cut out curtain and turn under a double ¾in (2cm) hem down both side edges. Pin in place, then turn under a double 2in (5cm) hem along base edge, mitering corners. Tack and stitch hems.
▪ Iron a 2in (5cm) strip of interfacing to right side of curtain at top, ⅜in (1cm) down from raw

canopy, curtains and cover

53

BEDROOM PAGEANTRY

edge of fabric. Fold and press fabric over top edge of interfacing, then bring folded edge over to form a double 2in (5cm) hem. Pin, tack and topstitch in place.

▪ Loops are spaced evenly at intervals of about 6in (15cm) apart. For each loop cut two pieces of contrast fabric measuring 3¼in × 9¼in (8cm × 23cm). With right sides together, pin, tack and stitch around the edges, leaving a small opening. Trim and turn to right side. Turn in opening edges and slipstitch to close.

▪ Work buttonholes at either end of each loop, centering them, and positioning them 1in (2.5cm) up from ends. At each loop position on curtain, stitch a button to both sides of the hemmed edge, 1in (2.5cm) from top and bottom edges of hem.

▪ To hang, button each loop to the back of the curtain, take it over the dowel and then button it to the front.

THE DUVET COVER AND PILLOWCASES

▪ Cut fabrics as follows: for duvet front cut one piece 81¼in × 82¼in (203cm × 205.5cm) from the larger fabric, and one piece 81¼in × 57½in (203cm × 146.5cm) for flap, from same fabric but with pattern running crosswise. For duvet back, cut one piece 81¼in (203cm) square from second main fabric. For each pillowcase, cut two pieces, one from main fabric and one from contrast, each 31¼in × 21¼in (78cm × 53cm).

▪ Fold flap section in half widthways so that folded piece measures 57½in × 40⅝in (146.5cm × 101.5cm). Mark a point 22⅝in (56.5cm) down raw side edges and draw a line from here up to the folded center. Cut along this line through both layers of fabric, then unfold fabric.

▪ Cut and join 4¾in (11cm) wide strips of contrast fabric to make a piece long enough to bind the pointed edge. Fold in ⅝in (1.5cm) along both long edges and press well. Unfold.

▪ Place strip to right side of flap with pressed seamline 1½in (4cm) from raw edge of flap. Pin, tack and stitch, taking ⅝in (1.5cm) seam allowance. Turning in other pressed edge of binding, bring binding over flap edge to cover previous seamline. Topstitch in place.

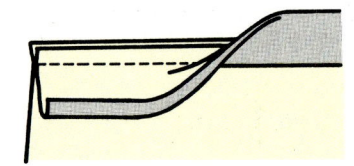

▪ Work 16 buttonholes, eight on each side of pointed center, at evenly spaced intervals along the band.

▪ Turn over and sew a double ¾in (2cm) hem along top edge of main front piece. Place flap on front cover, with raw edge projecting ⅝in (1.5cm) beyond hemmed edge. Mark positions of buttons on front cover and stitch in place. Fasten buttons through buttonholes.

▪ Tack front pieces together at overlapping sides. Place front on back, right sides together. Pin, tack and stitch all around, taking care to leave hemmed edge at top of main front piece free. Stitch again ⅛in (3cm) beyond first row of stitching. Trim and finish seam allowances together. Turn completed cover right side out.

▪ Take pillowcase pieces and bind one raw short edge of each piece with an 4¾in (11cm) wide strip of contrast fabric, following the same method as for duvet.

▪ For each pillowcase, take two contrasting pieces and join them together along the two long edges and unbound short edge, using French seams (see page 6). Mark and work six evenly spaced buttonholes along one bound edge then stitch buttons to inside of opposite bound edge to complete.

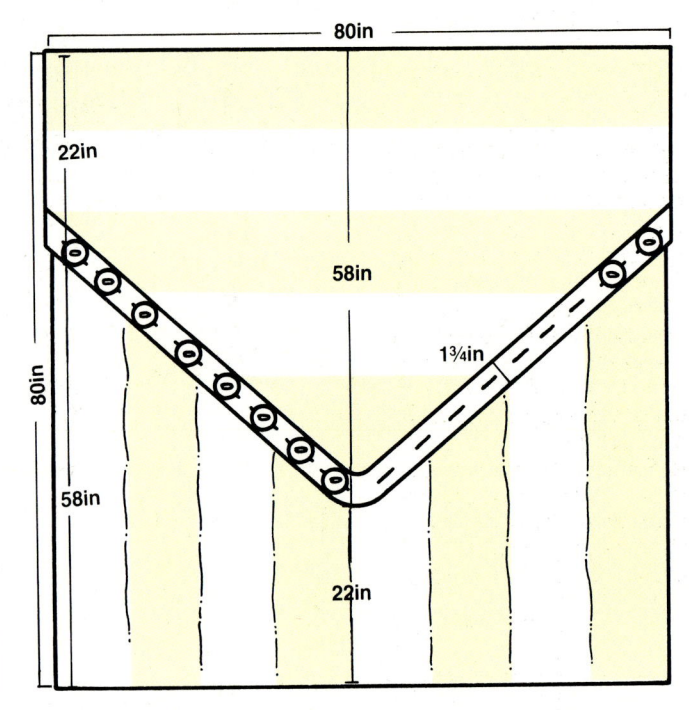

The measurements given show the dimensions of the completed cover. The binding must be eased around the point of the flap, turning it into a curve rather than a point. If you find it difficult to do this neatly, you may find it easier to make a mitered fold in the binding.

RUG TRANSFORMATION

If you are looking for something to brighten a corner of your room without going to enormous effort or expense, here is a comparatively quick way of adding your personal touch to a plain rug or mat and transforming it with a trelliswork and some scattered flowers. This simple pattern can easily be adapted to any size of rug, either by altering the scale or by simply extending the trellis in either direction, perhaps adding more random flowers.

Size: approximately 40in × 76in (100cm × 190cm) for quantities given.

MATERIALS

Woven rug in cotton or wool
Pingouin yarns in the following quantities and colors: Iceberg – two balls yellow 473 and one ball black 41; Pingostar – two balls gray 512 and one ball dark blue 528; Pingoland – one ball each of dark pink 822 and red 831; Tapis – one ball each of kingfisher 60 and emerald 35; Confortable sport – one ball bright pink 33
Large chenille needle
Tracing paper
Dressmakers' carbon paper
8in × 40in (20cm × 1m) strip of stiff card
Fine-tipped waterproof felt marker

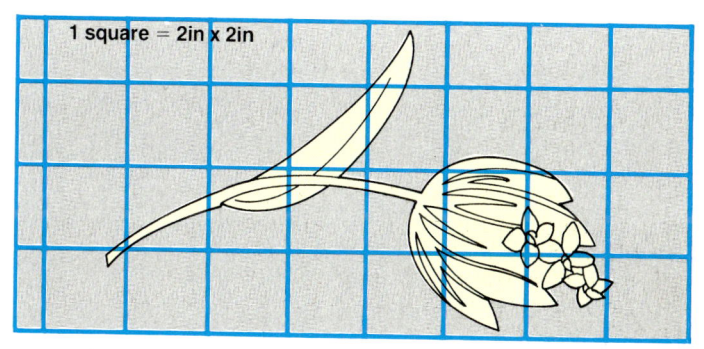

DIRECTIONS

▦ On reverse side of rug, mark a trellis of diagonal lines 8in (20cm) apart with the marker, using the strip of card as a guide.
▦ Enlarge the single flower pattern on tracing paper and, using dressmakers' carbon paper and turning the flower tracing different ways, transfer the complete pattern of scattered flowers to the right side of the rug.
▦ Embroider the flowers and leaves in long and short stitch and the gray stems and black pistils in overcast stitch as shown below, using the photograph as a color and stitch guide.
▦ Following the lines marked on the reverse of the rug, embroider the diagonal black lines in darning stitch, keeping each stitch approximately ⅜in (1cm) long.

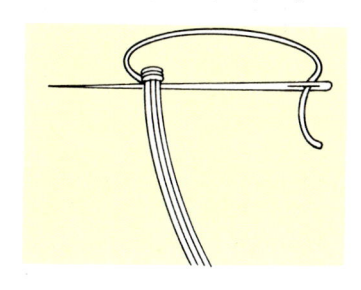

CRADLED IN COMFORT

Create a beautiful environment from which your baby can view the world with pleasure: whether you choose blue or pink, or play safe if you are a stickler for tradition, this pretty padded crib, complete with matching teddy, will be a wonderfully secure and cosy haven. The bag will prove invaluable for holding creams, cotton balls and other necessities, and if you have fabric – and energy – to spare you could make a tablecloth or even a nightdress to match. The crib will only last for a few months – an increasingly active baby will need something larger – but if the small scale and padded warmth help your baby to sleep soundly the effort will have been rewarded.

Sizes: crib approximately 47in × 24in (120cm × 60cm); bag 12in × 11½in (30cm × 29cm).

MATERIALS

FOR THE CRIB
4⅞in (4.4m) of 90in (228cm) wide printed sheeting
4⅞yd (4.7m) of 36in (90cm) wide medium-weight padding
1yd (1m) of 32in (80cm) wide buckram
4¾yd (4.7m) of 1in (2.5cm) wide ribbon
32in × 14in (80cm × 35cm) of ¼in (6mm) hardboard
31in × 14in (79cm × 35cm) cot mattress
1in (25mm) diameter dowel – four lengths each 47in (1200mm) long
2in × 1in (50mm × 25mm) planed beech – four lengths each 47in (1200mm) long
3yd (2.6m) of 2in (5cm) wide upholstery webbing
Eight 2in (50mm) long wood screws
Two 2½in (6cm) nuts and bolts, with washers
Sandpaper
Mat varnish

FOR THE BAG
⅝yd (50cm) of 90in (228cm) wide printed fabric
¾yd (60cm) of 36in (90cm) wide plastic fabric
⅝yd (50cm) of 36in (90cm) wide lightweight padding
Matching thread

FOR THE TEDDY
Scraps of printed fabric
Suitable filling
1yd (1m) of ⅜in (1cm) wide ribbon
Matching thread

DIRECTIONS

THE CRIB
▪ Round off the ends of the planed wood pieces with sandpaper. Varnish, sanding down between each coat.
▪ Drill a hole 1in (2.5cm) down from one end (the top) and another hole 3in (7.5cm) up from the other end of each piece. Also drill a hole for the bolt, 2in (5cm) above the center point of each piece, countersinking two of the pieces.
▪ Cross over the two pairs of end pieces, with the countersunk pieces on the outside, and fasten each pair with a nut and bolt, adding washers in between.
▪ Place dowel between crossed pieces, at the base of each piece, and screw in place. Repeat, to fit lengths of dowel at the top.
▪ Cut the webbing in half and join each piece to make two

baby blue coordinates

CRADLED IN COMFORT

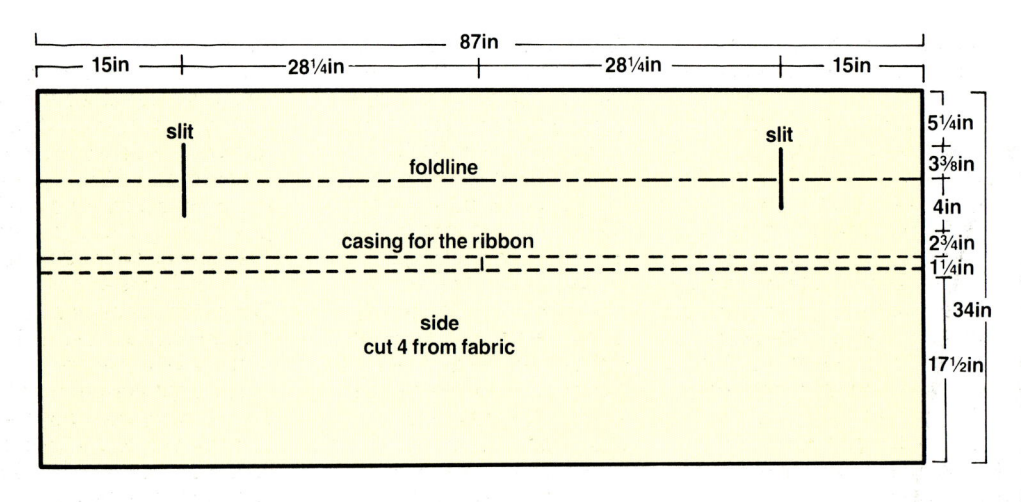

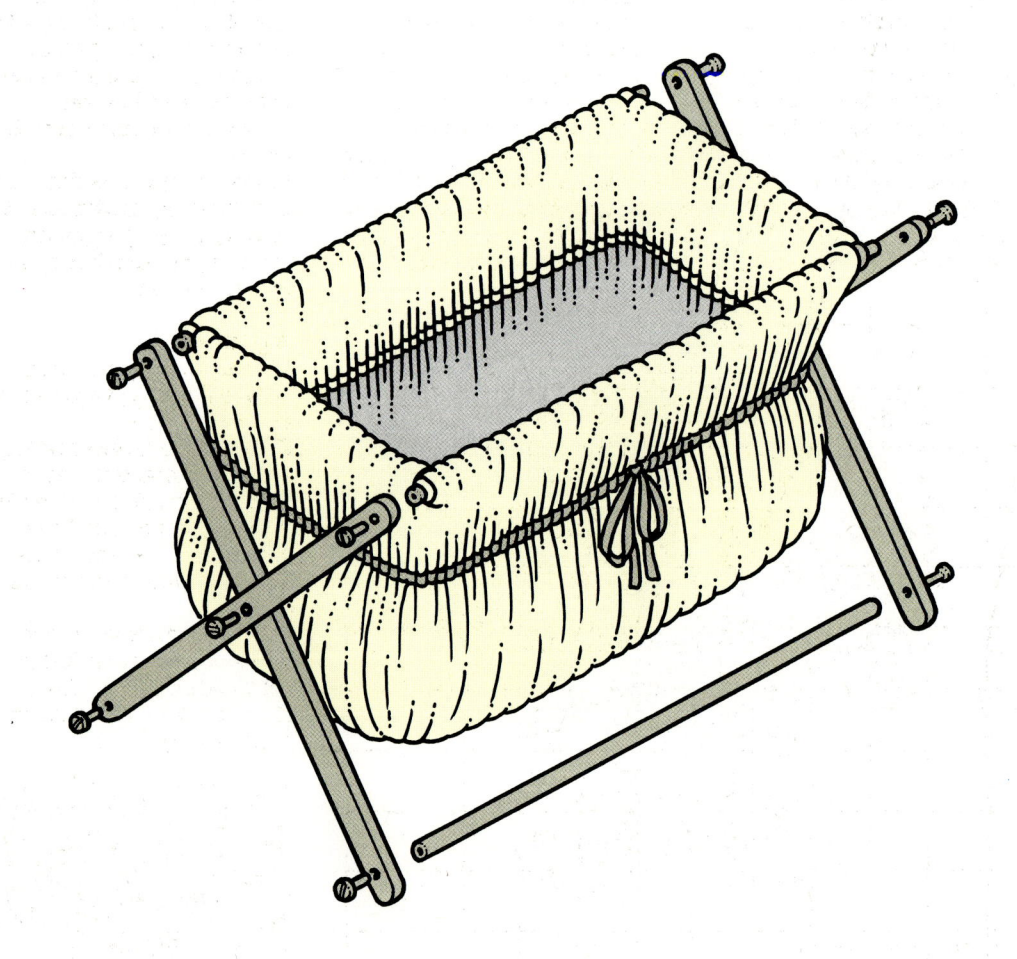

rings, each 48in (122cm) around, overlapping the ends and stitching very securely.

▥ Cut four pieces of sheeting each 87in × 34in (220cm × 86cm) for sides and two pieces each 33in × 15in (83cm × 38cm) for base. Also cut two sides 85¾in × 32¾in (217cm × 83cm) from padding and one base from buckram.

▥ Place the sides in pairs with right sides together and edges matching and join to make two rings. Lay the padding pieces flat, meeting end to end, and join with herringbone stitch down one short end. Turn over and herringbone stitch the other side, then join the other short ends in the same way, so that there are no bulky seams.

▥ Sandwich padding between the two fabric rings, right sides of fabric facing outwards. At the top, turn the fabric seam allowances in to meet each other, enclosing the padding, and either slipstitch or machine topstitch together.

▥ Pin and tack the three layers of the side piece thoroughly, then machine quilt lengthwise down the fabric in straight lines, spaced 2in (5cm) apart. With the fabric facing outwards and buckram sandwiched in the middle, stitch the base layers together around the outside, taking a ⅝in (1.5cm) seam allowance. Trim buckram back to seamline. Quilt the layers together as for the sides.

▥ Cut four slits in side where marked on the pattern. Bind each slit in the same way: cut two strips of fabric each 8in × 4in (20cm × 10cm). Fold each strip in half lengthwise, wrong sides together. Place a folded strip on each side of slit with raw edges facing inwards. On one side stitch the complete length of the slit. On

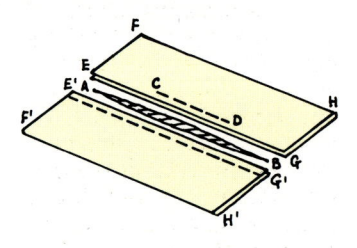

CRADLED IN COMFORT

the opposite side just stitch the central 4in (10cm) C to D. Turn strips through to the wrong side. Tack E-F to A-C. Fold the far end of the second strip onto the first strip matching E-F to E-C. Stitch E-F to E-C, then E-C to E-F. Repeat in the same way for G-H and G-H. This binds the slit for the cot frame both ways.

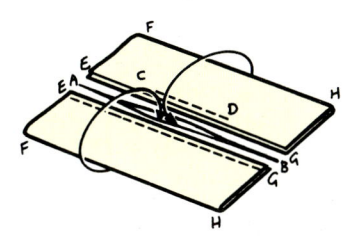

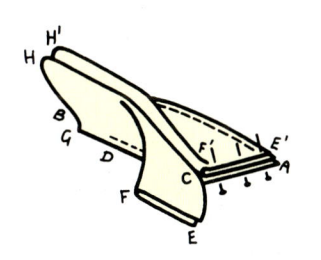

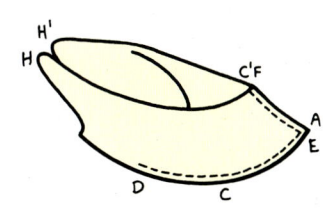

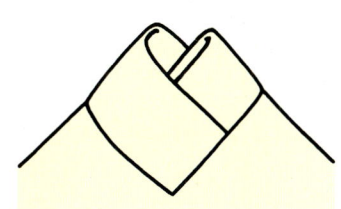

◻ Work a ¾in (2cm) vertical buttonhole in the center of one side, 17½in (44.5cm) up from the base edge, as shown.
◻ Turn over the top edge along the foldline and pin and tuck in position. Topstitch two rows of stitching, as shown, 1¼in (3cm) apart to form a casing.
◻ Work two rows of gathering stitches around the base edge of sides. Pull up gathers evenly to fit base. Join sides to base, gently rounding off the corners. Fold in raw edges of fabric to meet each other and topstitch along fold to finish.
◻ Thread ribbon around top casing and pull up till the top measures 118½in (300cm). Tie in a knot and then a bow.
◻ Push a webbing ring through each short end, bringing the ends of the ring through the openings. Unscrew the top dowel pieces of the cot and insert through the casing and through the ends of the webbing rings, then rescrew them in position.
◻ Place hardboard in cot to shape the base, then place mattress on top.

THE BAG
◻ From printed fabric cut out two pieces each 13in × 12½in (33cm × 32cm) for back and front, one piece 37in × 4¼in (92cm × 10.5cm) for the gusset. Repeat to cut out the same pieces from plastic. Also from plastic cut two pockets 12in × 6¾in (32cm × 17cm). From printed fabric cut two pieces for handles 16½in × 3¼in (42cm × 8cm). Cut out two pieces from padding each 11¾in × 11¼in (30cm × 29cm) and one piece 35¾in × 3in (89cm × 7.5cm).
◻ Center the padding pieces over the relevant fabric pieces, placing padding on the wrong side of the fabric and leaving a fabric margin of ⅝in (1.5cm) all around. Pin and tack together, tacking each way across the center first and then at intervals of about 4in (10cm). Using a machine straight stitch or a hand running stitch, quilt diagonally across the fabric both ways to quilt back, front and gusset in a diamond pattern, with the lines spaced 1½in (4cm) apart.
◻ Turn down the top edge of one pocket to form a double ⅜in (1cm) hem. Pin, tack and stitch hem. Repeat for second pocket.
◻ With wrong side of pocket to right side of plastic front and matching base edges and sides (to height of pocket sides), pin, tack and stitch pocket to plastic front. Repeat to stitch other pocket to plastic back.
◻ Take strips for handles and fold each in half lengthwise with right sides together. Pin, tack and stitch raw edges, leaving an opening at center of one side. Trim and turn to right side. Turn in opening edges in line with the remainder of the seam and slipstitch together to close. Topstitch all around each handle close to the edges.
◻ Place one handle on back and one on front fabric sections of bag: the handles should lie on the surface of the front or back, 3in (7.5cm) in from either side and with the raw ends of the handles projecting 1in (2.5cm) beyond the raw top edge of the fabric. Tack in place at fabric seamline.
◻ With right sides together, place plastic front over fabric front, enclosing handle, and stitch along top seamline, taking a ⅝in (1.5cm) seam allowance. Turn right side out, bringing up handle, and topstitch ¾in (2cm) below top edge. Tack plastic and fabric together along side and base. Repeat for bag back.
◻ With right sides together and taking a ⅝in (1.5cm) seam, stitch fabric and plastic gusset pieces together across the short ends. Turn right side out.
◻ Matching short edges of gusset to top edge of front, stitch front to gusset, taking a ⅝in (1.5cm) seam. Repeat to stitch back to gusset. Trim seam allowances back to a scant ¼in (6mm).
◻ Pinching gusset and front or back together, topstitch around seams joining bag to gusset, enclosing the raw edges on the inside of the bag.

THE TEDDY
◻ Draw up the pattern to the desired size and cut two pattern pieces from fabric.
◻ Place the two pieces with right sides together and pin, tack and stitch together all around, leaving an opening in one side. Stitch again, close to previous line of stitching. Trim and turn to right side.
◻ Fill the teddy firmly. Turn in opening edges in line with the seam and slipstitch to close.
◻ Tie a ribbon around teddy's neck, forming it into a bow.

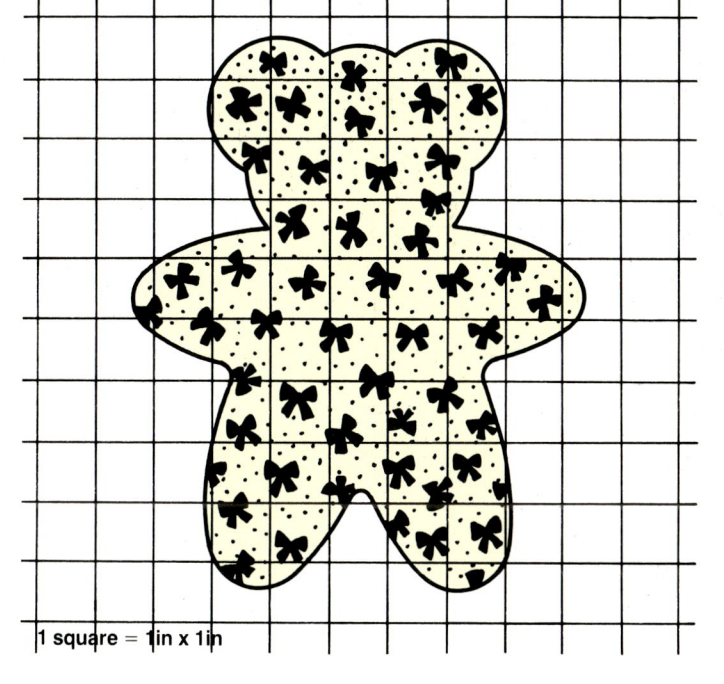

1 square = 1in × 1in

SPRINGTIME DREAM

This lavishly embroidered, luxuriously feminine bedcover, with its matching pillowcases, was inspired by four new varieties of tulip: Greenland, pink and tender green; Angélique, luscious as a peony; Shirley, ivory tinged with purple, and Dreaming Mead, with its lovely closed buds. You can either embroider the designs by hand, as seen in the picture, carefully blending the different shades like a skilled artist, or for quicker results you could machine embroider the flowers and leaves, using variegated threads. An even speedier method would be to paint the design, using fabric paints and taking care to make delicately shaded petals. The flowers, stems and leaves might be outlined in stem stitch and selected areas highlighted with satin stitching.

Size: bedcover 92in × 87in (230cm × 220cm); pillowcases 36in × 24¾in (90cm × 62cm), including scalloped edges.

MATERIALS

*4¼yd (3.8m) of 90in (228cm) wide fine cotton or linen fabric
DMC stranded cotton as follows: two skeins each of green 92, 369 and 703, and ecru; one skein each of green 94, 471, 472, 580, 966, 987, 989 and 3347, white, pink 62, 106, 112, 602, 603, 604, 760, 761, 776, 819, 892, 893, 948, 3326 and 3689, blue 828 and yellow 445
or machine embroidery cottons in variegated pinks and greens
or fabric paints and a range of paint brushes with green and pink stranded cottons for outlining the designs
2 reels of DMC machine embroidery cotton in pale pink No. 50, for scalloped edges of pillowcases
Pink colored pencil
Crewel needle size 7 or 8
Tracing paper
Dressmakers' carbon paper
Large embroidery hoop
Matching thread*
Note *If the above yarn is unobtainable, refer to page 80.*

tulips for collectors

DIRECTIONS

- Cut one piece of fabric 98in (246cm) long, cutting across the full width, for the bedcover. For the pillowcases, cut two pieces 36in × 24¾in (90cm × 62cm) for the tops and two pieces 36in × 20in (90cm × 50cm) for the bottoms.
- On the bedcover piece, make ¾in (2cm) double hems down the sides, and 1½in (4cm) double hems at the top and bottom.
- Starting from the corners measure out evenly spaced scallops around the edges of the pillowcase tops and draw them on the fabric in colored pencil. Embroider the scallops in pink machine embroidery cotton, using machine satin stitch 3/16in (4mm) wide.
- Enlarge the design for the bedcover onto tracing paper and transfer it to the cover with dressmakers' carbon paper (see page 6), using the photograph as a guide to position.
- Transfer the pillowcase design to the pillowcase tops in the same manner.
- Embroider the tulip motifs in long and short stitch, using the charts as color guides and the photograph as a stitch guide. Two strands of thread are used throughout and the stitches should be between 1/8in (3mm) and 3/16in (4mm) long to achieve the painted effect shown on the photograph. Work with the fabric stretched in an embroidery hoop, moving it as necessary.
- If you wish to work the design in machine embroidery, first stitch the main outlines by hand in stem stitch. Then put the fabric in a small embroidery hoop: lay the fabric right side up over the outer ring, then place the inner ring over it, so the fabric can lie flat on the base plate of your machine. Set the machine to straight running stitch and make the feed inoperative so that you can move the ring freely until each area is filled with stitching. The speed with which you move the ring about will govern the length of the stitches, so practise first.
- When the embroidery is complete, place it face downwards on a well padded surface and press it lightly, taking care not to crush the stitches.
- To complete the pillowcases, for each pillowcase take an bottom section and make 3/8in (1cm) double hems down all four sides. Bring over a 4¾in (12cm) deep fold of fabric to the wrong side across one short end and tack at the sides.
- With wrong sides together, center bottom section over pillowcase top, taking care that scalloped edges extend evenly all around. Pin and tack together, then topstitch or stabstitch along the two long sides and the unfolded short end. Remove tacking and insert pillow, tucking it under the flap.

SPRINGTIME DREAM

Enlarge to twice this size (see page 6).

Enlarge to twice this size (see page 6).

62

SPRINGTIME DREAM

Enlarge to twice this size (see page 6).

KEY

Top left
- **a** 948
- **b** 112
- **c** 106
- **d** 62
- **e** 776
- **f** 761
- **g** 760
- **h** 893
- **i** 892
- **j** 3326
- **k** 819
- **l** white
- **m** 369
- **n** 989
- **o** 987
- **p** 472
- **q** 966
- **r** 92

Bottom left
- **a** 602
- **b** 603
- **c** 604
- **d** 819
- **e** 776
- **f** ecru
- **g** 369
- **h** white
- **i** 828
- **j** 948
- **k** 989
- **l** 987
- **m** 445
- **n** 472
- **o** 966
- **p** 92

Above
- **a** ecru
- **b** white
- **c** 3326
- **d** 3347
- **e** 369
- **f** 819
- **g** 776
- **h** 471
- **i** 3689
- **j** 948
- **k** 760
- **l** 761
- **m** 604
- **n** 471
- **o** 94
- **p** 703
- **q** 92
- **r** 603
- **s** 472
- **t** 966
- **u** 580

63

LACED HEADBOARD

The simplest ideas are often the most successful, like this elegantly sporty headboard – a complete contrast to the more usual, highly padded variety, and much more in keeping with those who like their living spaces to be practical, uncluttered and stylish, but with a light touch of humor. The cover is so easy to make – just two rectangles of calico, one laced over the other – that you could sew it in an evening.

Size: the cover can be made to fit any rectangular headboard.

MATERIALS

36in (90cm) wide calico – quantity will vary according to the height of the headboard: approximately 3¼yd (3m) for a 4ft 6in (135cm) wide bed and 2½yd (2m) for a 3ft (90cm) wide bed
White cord – approximately 5yd (4.5m) for a 4ft 6in (135cm) wide bed and 3¼yd (3m) for a 3ft (90cm) wide bed
1⅝yd (1.5m) of ½in (13mm) wide white tape
¼in (6mm) diameter white eyelets and an eyelet punch
Matching thread
1in (2.5cm) thick foam, cut to the size of the headboard
All purpose adhesive

DIRECTIONS

▦ If you do not have a rectangular headboard, cut plywood to the desired size. Also check that the board can be fixed to the bed. Using adhesive, fix foam to the front of headboard.

▦ Measure the headboard both ways. For the back, cut a rectangle of cotton to this size, adding the headboard thickness plus 7½in (19cm) to the length and twice the headboard thickness plus 12in (30cm) to the width. For the front, cut a piece to the headboard measurement plus the headboard thickness and ⅜in (1cm) on the length and less 2½in (6cm) on the width.

▦ Finish the side and top edges of the front with zigzag stitches and turn these edges under for 2in (5cm). Pin and tack. Turn up the lower edge to make a double ¾in (2cm) hem; pin, tack and stitch.

▦ Turn under top and side edges of back piece for 2in (5cm) and press. Unfold. Turn under and stitch a double ¾in (2cm) hem at lower edge.

▦ Center the back piece over the back of the headboard, bringing sides and top over to the front (lower edge is level with lower edge of board). Pin to hold. Fold in top corner points, then turn in top and side edges to form mitered corners. Pin corners, then remove back from headboard and stitch mitered corners up to pressed lines 2in (5cm) from front edges.

▦ Turn under top and side edges along pressed lines and tack.

▦ Pin front and back together over headboard, with back overlapping front at top and side edges by ¾in (2cm). Mark positions for eyelets on top and side edges, 1in (2.5cm) from inner edges on back and 1¾in (4.5cm) from outer edges on front. Place eyelets about 4in (10cm) apart on each edge, and stagger the positions so that the cord will run at an angle.

▦ Remove and unpin both sections and punch eyelets in place through folded thicknesses of fabric (this will hold hems in place). Also position two eyelets at both sides of mitered corner.

▦ Cut tape into eight equal lengths and stitch to lower edges of cover at matching positions to make four pairs of ties.

▦ Replace front and back over headboard and, beginning at the base edge, lace the two pieces together, tucking the front section under the back for ¾in (2cm). At opposite edge, pull cord and knot behind last eyelet.

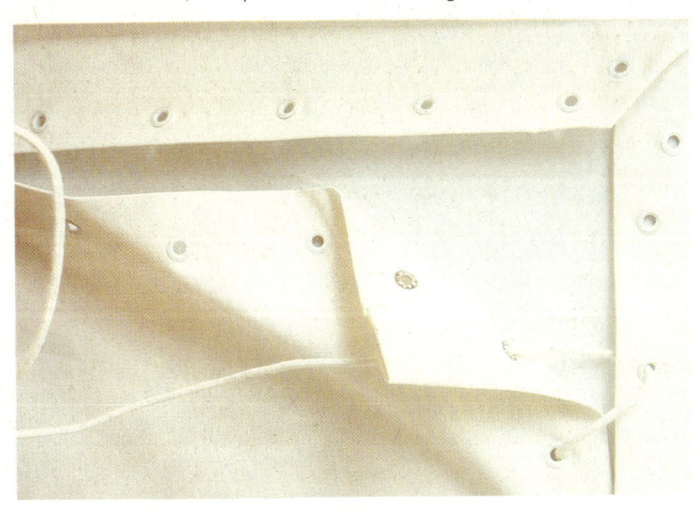

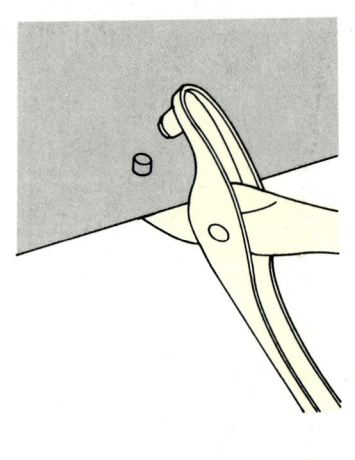

stylish and sporty

SUNNY DAYS

Enhance the joys of summer – the long hot days, the long cool drinks and the lazy chatter of friends – with a charming and elegant deckchair and matching parasol. Choose the prettiest chintz you can find for the chair cover, then copy one of the motifs onto a plain parasol: the idea is so simple, yet so perfect a way to set a summer scene. If you are not sure whether your upholstery fabric is quite strong enough for a deckchair, back it according to the instructions given below.

MATERIALS

FOR THE DECKCHAIR COVER
Printed cotton fabric – see below for quantity
Plain white cotton fabric (as above)
Iron-on interfacing
Matching thread
Upholstery nails or heavy-duty staples
Deckchair

FOR THE PARASOL
Tracing paper
Dressmakers' carbon paper
Oiled stencil board
Craft knife
Fabric paints
Adhesive tape
Stencil brush or small piece of sponge
Large plain white umbrella or parasol

DIRECTIONS

THE DECKCHAIR COVER
◼ Lay the deckchair flat and measure across the top or bottom fixing bar. Add 5in (12cm) to this to find the width. Cut printed fabric to this width and sufficiently long to wrap around the fixing bars and fasten. Cut white cotton to the same size.
◼ Match the two fabrics with wrong sides together; pin and tack together all around the outer edge. Make up the cover treating the two fabrics as one piece.
◼ Cut a 1¼in (3cm) wide strip of iron-on interfacing the length of each side of cover. Lay on wrong side against the outer edge at both sides of the cover and iron in place. Turn over a double 1¼in (3cm) wide hem along each side edge. Pin, tack and stitch both hems in place, stitching close to both edges for strength.
◼ Turn under both short ends and fasten to the deckchair frame with upholstery nails or heavy-duty staples.

66

elegant deckchair set

SUNNY DAYS

THE PARASOL
- Trace off a motif from the printed fabric, simplifying the design if necessary for the stencil outline. Stems and fine details of shading can be painted in freehand afterwards.
- If you have never tried stencilling before, keep to a relatively simple, clearly defined outline. A single, large-scale motif would in any case be more effective on a large parasol than an intricately detailed pattern. If you are not sure how the completed motif will look, make a sample painting on fabric before cutting the stencil. To do this, use your final tracing (see bottom left picture) and dressmaker's carbon paper to copy the outline onto a spare piece of fabric, then color it in with fabric paints.
- Place the finished stencil against the open parasol and hold it with adhesive tape. Using a small piece of sponge or a stencil brush, dab the paint over the stencil.
- When the paint has dried, remove the stencil and mark the next section. Fill in any extra details such as leaf veins, by hand, using a fine brush.
- If necessary (see manufacturer's instructions) fix the paint to the fabric with a hot iron.
- For a finishing touch, make yourself a straw hat to match: take an ordinary straw hat with a wide brim; cut out a motif from the fabric, leaving a margin of ¼in (6mm) all around. Turn under and tack the seam allowance, then slipstitch the motif to the hat. Alternatively, use adhesive fabric to set the motif in position.

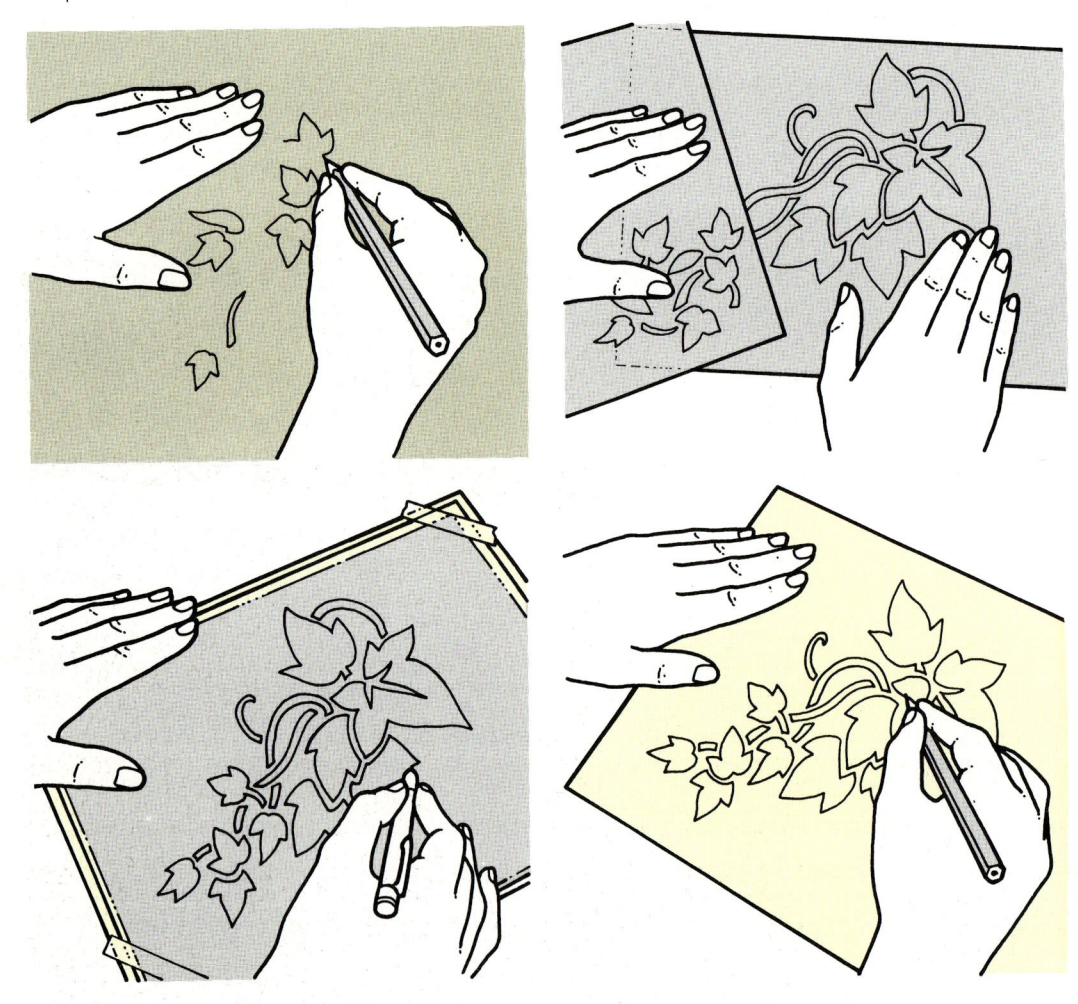

Top left *Place the fabric on a flat surface, smoothing out any wrinkles. Place adhesive tape at the corners to hold it firm. Using a soft pencil, trace isolated motifs. Simplify the shapes, if necessary, to achieve clearly defined outlines.*
Top right *Once you have traced all the motifs, cut them out from tracing paper so that you can move the pieces around to create a pleasing arrangement.*
Bottom left *Trace the arrangement, then place carbon paper between the tracing and the board. Tape the tracing in position and go over the lines with a ball-point pen.*
Bottom right *Make any final improvements to the stencil with a pencil, then cut out the shapes with a craft knife.*

SUNNY DAYS

CELEBRATION TIME

Clouds of net, as light and airy as champagne bubbles and decorated with feathers, ribbons and tiny balls, create a magical party scene for Christmas, a birthday, an engagement, a wedding anniversary or whatever you choose. If you are too inhibited even to dine by candlelight, this is not for you, but if you share the Gallic love for the dramatic and for creating a romantic or festive atmosphere, then you will appreciate this instant transformation.

Sizes: to fit your own requirements.

MATERIALS

FOR THE DOOR CURTAIN
Net fabric – see below for quantity
Small amounts of plain cotton fabric for appliqué
Chenille braid
¾in (2cm) diameter polystyrene balls
Fabric adhesive
Bodkin
Matching thread

FOR THE LAMPSHADE COVER
Net fabric – see below for quantity
Chenille braid
¾in (2cm) diameter polystyrene balls
Fabric adhesive
Matching thread

FOR THE CLOTH
Net fabric – see below for quantity
Chenille braid
Feathers
Fabric adhesive
Matching thread

DIRECTIONS

THE DOOR CURTAIN
▨ Measure the door and cut a length of net fabric to this size, plus 1in (2cm) on the width and 3in (7cm) on the length, for top casing and hems.
▨ Turn under a double ¼in (6mm) wide hem on side and base edges of curtain, making neat base corners. Pin, tack and stitch hems in place.
▨ At the top edge, turn under a double 1¼in (3mm) wide hem to form a casing; pin, tack and stitch in place along the lower folded edge.
▨ Using fabric adhesive, fix braid haphazardly over the curtain in a loopy design, adding polystyrene balls. Push a hole straight through the center of each ball with a bodkin and push in the folded braid, till the end just comes through on the opposite side.
▨ Add appliqué shapes: decide on a simple flower and leaf design and mark the shapes onto the fabric. Stitch round each shape just inside the outline. Cut out each shape. Pin appliqué shapes onto the curtain, set your sewing-machine to a close zigzag stitch and work around each shape. Add trails of braid for stamens.
▨ Thread on covered wire and hang above the door.

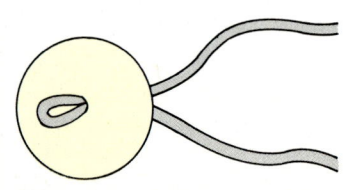

THE LAMPSHADE
▨ Measure from the center of the top of the existing lampshade to the desired length of the cover and cut out a square to twice this length.
▨ Turn up a tiny hem to the right side and handstitch in place with small stitches. With edge of braid butting the outer edge of net, glue braid over edge of cover, adding polystyrene balls at intervals, as for the door curtain.
▨ Cut a 2in (5cm) diameter hole

70

setting the scene

from the center of the square. Finish the edge by adding braid in the same way as the hem edge.
▦ Add random patterns of braid all over the square.
▦ Place the net cover over the existing lampshade. Make sure that your lampshade will keep the net at a safe distance from the light bulb, so that there is no danger that it might catch fire, and use a low wattage bulb. Never try to cover a live flame, even if the distance between the flame and the net seems safe.

THE CLOTH
▦ Cut a square of fabric to the desired size and finish the outer edge as for the lampshade.
▦ Work tiny bars in the cloth at positions chosen for the feathers. Slot the feathers through the bars to hold them in place (in this way they can easily be removed when you need to wash the cloth).

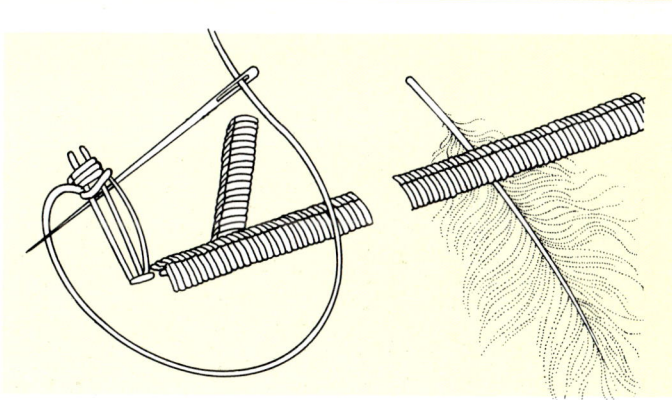

PATCHWORK CURTAIN

Sunlight filtering through a white cotton curtain, illuminating patches of chintz scattered with flowers, birds or butterflies, like little scenes in a stained glass window – what could be prettier? Some patchwork techniques can be rather time consuming, but here is a way of achieving the charm and character of a traditional patchwork by using a very quick and easy machine method. Drape the finished piece over a pole or make it into a conventional curtain.

Size: to fit your own requirements.

MATERIALS

Plain white cotton fabric to desired size
Assortment of floral-patterned cotton fabrics for appliqué
Matching threads
Pair of sharp-pointed embroidery scissors

DIRECTIONS

▧ Decide on the finished size of the curtain and cut out one piece of plain white cotton fabric to this size, adding 1½in (4cm) on the width and 5¾in (14cm) to the length for hem and top.
▧ Turn under a double ⅜in (1cm) hem on both side edges. Turn under a double 2½in (6cm) hem on base edge, making neat base corners. Pin, tack and stitch all around. Turn under and stitch a double ⅜in (1cm) hem along top edge.
▧ Press the curtain to eliminate all the creases and lay flat on a large work surface right side up.
▧ From the chosen appliqué fabrics cut out squares and rectangles in different sizes, ranging from about 3in (7.5cm) to 10in (25cm) either way. In some cases two or more fabrics can be stitched together with plain flat seams to form multi-colored sections. Mark, then cut out each piece, allowing for a margin all around of about ¾in (2cm).
▧ Position all the appliqué pieces right side up on the right side of the curtain and move them about until the desired effect is reached, then pin and tack in place. Vertically tack large pieces to the background to keep them flat. 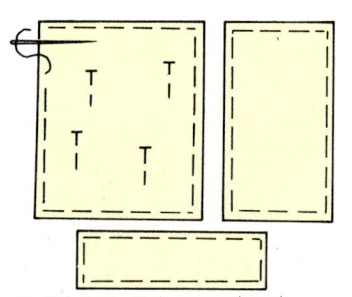
▧ Straight stitch around each piece along the marked outline and fasten off securely. Using a pair of sharp-pointed embroidery scissors, cut away the allowance from around each piece very close to the stitching line. Take care not to cut through the stitches. 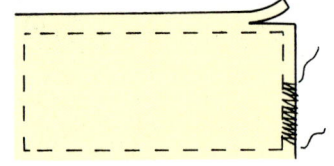
▧ Set the sewing-machine to a zigzag stitch. Before stitching, test the stitch on a spare piece of fabric and adjust the stitch size if necessary. Stitch around each piece in turn. After stitching pull all the working threads through to the wrong side and fasten off. Remove the tacking stitches and press.
▧ Hang the curtain draped over a curtain pole beside the bed.

sunlit scenery

LAZY DAYS

There are few better ways of unwinding and relaxing than to swing lazily to and fro in a hammock on a warm summer's day, and this particular version, with its bright creole colors and attractive braided ties, makes a lovely garden ornament even when it is not in use. Choose a good, strong fabric and check before buying that the weft threads can easily be removed. Pulling out the threads can be a time consuming business but it is very simple and there is no reason why all the potential users of the hammock, children included, should not join in its making.

Size: approximately 64in × 60in (160cm × 150cm), excluding braids.

MATERIALS

4½yd (4m) of 60in (150cm) wide woven cotton fabric
52in (1300mm) length of 1½in (40mm) diameter dowel
1½yd (1.4m) of 1in (2.5cm) wide webbing
Tacks
Cotton yarn in a toning color
Two painted wood napkin rings, purchased to fit after plaiting is complete
⅜in (15mm) tacks
Matching thread

DIRECTIONS

▪ Mark the center of the fabric, then mark 32in (80cm) on both sides of the center. Work two rows of zigzag stitching across the fabric width at these points.
▪ Unravel all the weft threads from both ends of the fabric, beyond the lines of the zigzag stitching.
▪ Divide the loose strands into bunches of about sixty strands and temporarily hold – make sure that the bunches look the same.
▪ Working with a bunch at a time, divide the bunch into three even sections and work together in a conventional three-strand braid to the end of the strands. Temporarily hold the end with a rubber band. Cut an 32in (80cm) length of yarn and hold the end against the end of the braid, bind the remaining yarn round the end of the braid, covering the yarn end as well as the strand ends. Thread the end of the yarn back through the binding.
▪ Turn under the selvage for ⅜in (1cm) on each side of the center section; pin, tack and stitch in place.
▪ Cut one length of dowel 40in (1000mm) long and two pieces each 6in (150mm) long. Drill a 1in (25mm) hole centrally in each 6in (150mm) piece. Measure the distance across the short piece and mark this length on each end of longer piece. Shave down both ends to the marks so they will fit snugly into the holes. Gently hammer in place.
▪ Gather all the braids together at one side and push through a napkin ring. Thread one end of webbing through the ring. Wind the webbing over the dowel end and hammer tacks firmly in place to hold. Knot braids around T-shaped end, to hold securely. Repeat at opposite side of bar.

colorful hammock

COLORFUL HARMONY

Little finishing touches often make all the difference to a beautiful decor: a few flowers in a vase, echoing the colors of the walls or furnishings, a pretty sofa throw or, in this case, bands of bright, shining satin ribbon, rippling over the damask background of cushions, duvet cover, tablecloth and curtains. Instantly, a scheme which would already have been pretty if the fabrics had been left undecorated becomes something beautiful and much more inspired.

Sizes: cushions 18in × 10¼in (45cm × 26cm); duvet cover 55in × 80in (140cm × 200cm); tablecloth 46½in × 46½in (118cm × 118cm); cafe curtains to fit your window measurements.

MATERIALS

FOR EACH CUSHION
⅜yd (30cm) of 48in (120cm) wide damask
¾in (2cm) wide ribbon in different colors for border and appliqué
18½in × 10¾in (46.5cm × 27cm) cushion pad
Matching threads

FOR THE DUVET COVER
2½yd (2.2m) of 48in (120cm) wide yellow damask
2½yd (2.2m) of 48in (120cm) wide pink damask
¾in (2cm) wide ribbon in different colors for appliqué
1yd (1m) of snap tape
Matching threads

FOR THE TABLECLOTH
1¼yd (1.2m) of 48in (120cm) wide damask
¾in (2cm) wide ribbon in different colors for border and appliqué
Matching threads

FOR THE CAFE CURTAINS
48in (120cm) wide damask (see below for quantity)
¾in (2cm) wide ribbon in different colors for border, appliqué and hanging loops
Matching threads

DIRECTIONS

FOR EACH CUSHION
■ Cut out two pieces of damask each 19¼in × 11½in (48cm × 29cm).
■ On cushion front arrange 4in (10cm) lengths of ribbon, either running in parallel lines or crossed: the choice is yours. When the arrangement looks good, pin and tack in place. Set your sewing-machine to a close zigzag stitch and test on a small scrap of fabric before stitching. Stitch all around each piece of ribbon, working the long sides in the same direction to avoid wrinkles.
■ Mark a ⅝in (1.5cm) seam allowance all around cushion front with tacking stitches. Lay a border ribbon around the outer edge, butting the outer edge of the ribbon up against the tacked line and mitering each corner. Begin and end behind one mitered corner. Pin, tack and topstitch the ribbon in place.
■ With right sides together, pin, tack and stitch cushion front to cushion back, leaving a center opening in one side. Trim and turn through to the right side.
■ Insert cushion pad. Turn in opening edges in line with the remainder of the seam and slipstitch together to close.

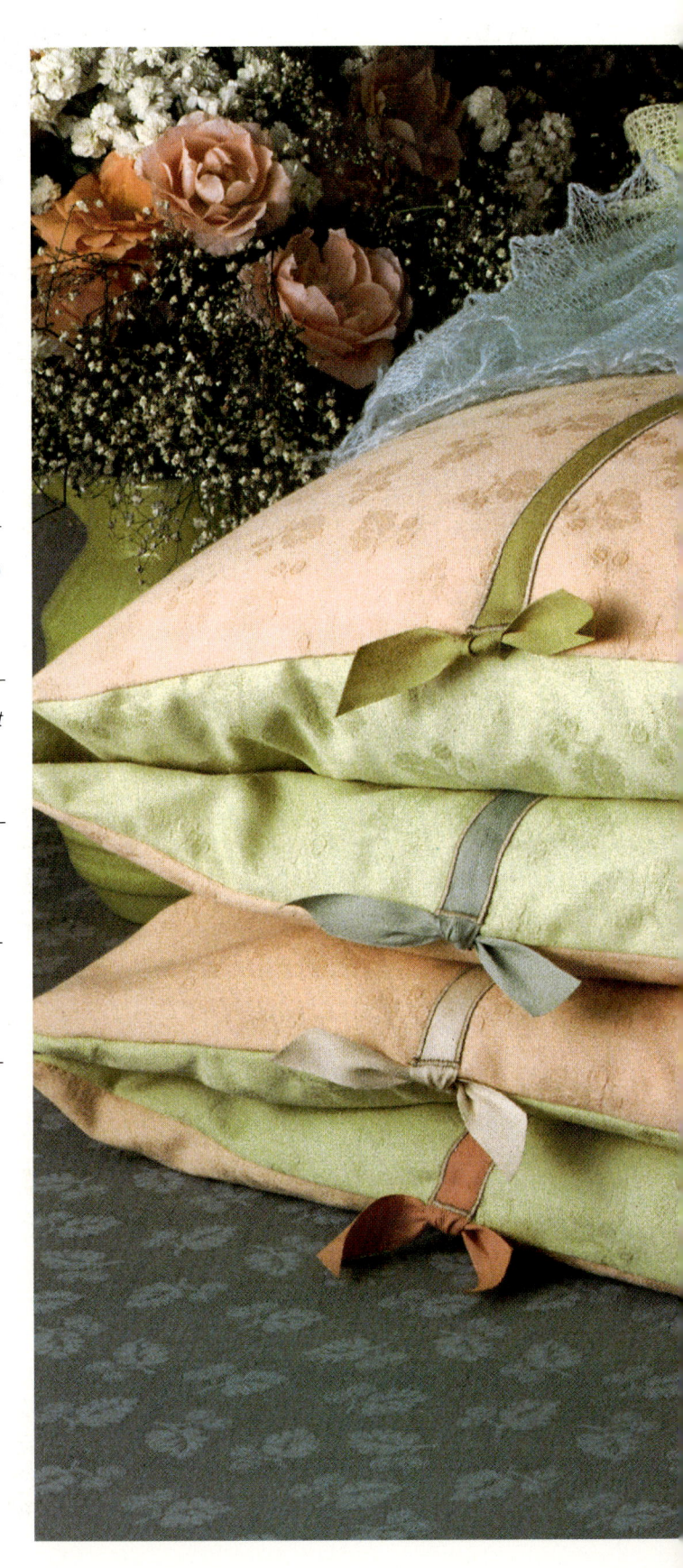

ribbons for a beautiful home

COLORFUL HARMONY

THE DUVET COVER
- One side of the cover is yellow and the other is pink. Both sides are made from four pieces of fabric, two plain and two with ribbon appliqué. From yellow fabric cut two pieces each 41¼in × 27½in (103cm × 73cm) for top (headboard) quarters and two pieces each 42½in × 27½in (106.5cm × 73cm) for base quarters (the extra length includes an allowance for the fastening). Cut pieces the same size from pink fabric, for the other side of the cover.
- Decorate one top and one base section for each side: position two strips of ribbon across the width, spacing them equally from each other and the seamline, and one strip across the length. Pin and tack each strip in place. Set your machine to a close zigzag stitch and test on a spare piece of fabric before stitching. Stitch along all edges of each length of ribbon, stitching across short ends just inside the seamline.
- Pin, tack and stitch appliquéd pieces to plain pieces in pairs, along one long edge.
- Pin, tack and stitch yellow top pieces to yellow base pieces and pink top pieces to pink base pieces, with appliquéd sections at opposite corners.
- Fold a double 1in (2.5cm) wide hem along base edge of each piece; pin, tack and stitch. Place cover pieces with right sides together, matching hem edges; pin, tack and stitch hem edges together for 12in (30cm) in from either side, leaving a center opening.
- Pin, tack and stitch press snap tape into each side of the opening, so that the snaps match. Stitch across each end of the opening.
- Complete the duvet cover with French seams, stitching the sides first and then the top edges.
- To complete, stitch ribbon bows to ends of appliqué ribbon at the outer edges of the cover.

78

COLORFUL HARMONY

THE TABLECLOTH

◼ Turn up a ⅜in (1cm) hem to the right side of the fabric, all around the outer edge. Pin and tack, making neat corners. Position the ribbon around the edge, with the outer edge of the ribbon just covering the raw edges of the fabric. Miter the corners of the ribbon. Pin, tack and topstitch.

◼ Add other bands of ribbon and 4in (10cm) lengths of ribbon appliqué in the same way as for the cushion covers.

THE CAFE CURTAIN

◼ Measure the height of your window and decide how deep you wish your finished curtain to be: it could cover only half the window, or the full length, allowing for a gap at the top for loops. Cut fabric to the desired finished depth plus 5½in (14cm), and to the pole width plus 1½in (4cm) for each side hem.

◼ Turn under a double ¾in (2cm) hem at both side edges and pin. Turn under and pin a double 2in (5cm) hem at the lower edge and a double ¾in (2cm) hem at the top. Miter all corners, then stitch hems all around curtain.

◼ Position a border of ribbon all around the curtain, 1in (2.5cm) from outer edge, mitering the corners. Position ribbon ends underneath a mitered corner. Pin, tack and topstitch in place, stitching along both edges.

◼ Position inner rows of ribbon in two different colors and stitch in the same way. Add lengths of appliquéd ribbon, as for cushions.

◼ Work with two different colors of ribbon to provide the hanging loops along the top edge; attach the first ribbon behind the outer edge. Tack along the back of the curtain at 3¼in (8cm) intervals, forming 1½in (4cm) loops as shown. Pin the folded ribbon in place at the back. Stitch in place.

◼ Repeat with the second colored ribbon, making loops of the same size and centering them between the first set.

◼ Tie the two ends together at the side. Slide the curtain onto the pole.

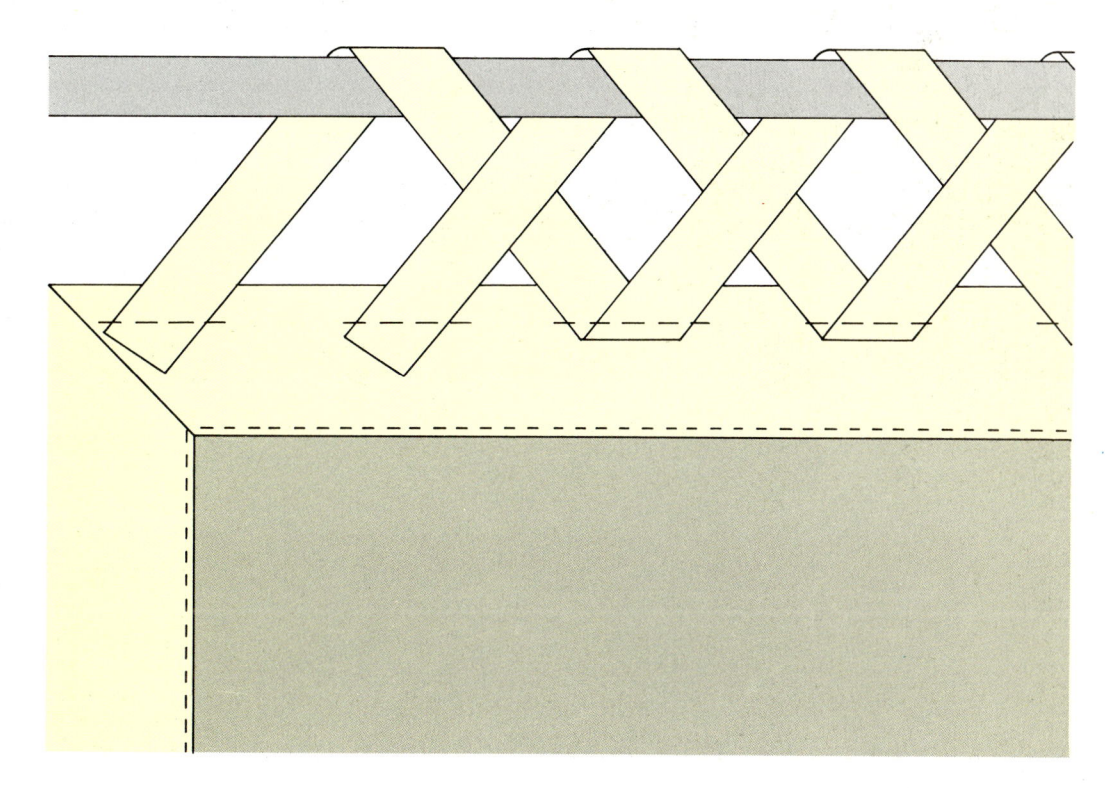

STOCKISTS

DMC Yarns
DMC Corporation 107 Trumbull Street
Elizabeth NJ 07206 (201) 351-4550

Mail order companies:

Anchor Yarns
Susan Bates, Inc. 212 Middlesex Avenue
Chester, CT 06412 (203) 526-5381

Merino Wool Co., Inc.
230 Fifth Avenue New York NY 10001 (212) 686-0050

Pingouin Yarns
P.O. Box 100 Jamestown SC 29453 1-800-845-2291